The Naked Children

If language is the clothing of life,
no child should be sent
naked into the world.

The

Naked
Children

Daniel Fader

The Macmillan Company, New York, New York
Collier-Macmillan Limited, London

Part One

✿◇✿◇✿◇✿◇✿◇✿◇✿◇✿◇✿◇

This is the story of one school year in the life of Cleo, Wentworth, Snapper, Rubbergut, and Uncle Wiggly. Thirteen and fourteen years old in the 1965–1966 academic year, eighth and ninth grade students in Washington's Garnet-Patterson Junior High School, organized and led by Cleo, the only girl—they were my companions, my friends, and my colleagues. They were also the single most powerful force I have ever known for good change in bad education. This book is written in celebration of their work and in gratitude for the many gifts they gave me.

Introduction

I WROTE to Carl Hansen, then Superintendent of Schools in the District of Columbia, asking him for use of a school to continue an experiment in education. With my letter I sent a description and some preliminary findings of a new approach to teaching literacy then being tested at Maxey Boys Training School in Whitmore Lake, Michigan. Hansen's answer was an invitation to come to Washington to talk with him and his staff.

A large group of schoolmen and women, including the Superintendent, awaited me. All had read the materials I sent; some had questions: Could the program be transferred to a public school and adapted to the requirements of coeducation? (Yes, in both cases.) Didn't I believe in the value of teaching fine literature? (Sometimes, to some children.) Would I be willing to direct the District's installation of the program, and what would be the cost of my services? My answer to the last weighed heavily in my favor: The U. S. Office of Education was interested in observing transfer of the program called "English in Every Classroom" from a penal to a public school. They would pay my salary and expenses if I came from Michigan to install the program myself.

Federal funds and the University of Michigan together? I could have the nineteen schools of the Model School Division, an administrator's nightmare composed of schools with the most difficult educational problems. But would nineteen schools form a group large enough for my purposes?

It would, I said, be somewhat larger than the number I had in mind—eighteen schools larger, to be exact. I was amazed by their response to a program barely a year old in the training school, with little more than my enthusiasm and its persuasiveness on paper to recommend it. I had begun to learn a lesson about urban public schools in the United States: Any change is good; visible change is better; visible, inexpensive change is best.

Thank you for your generosity, I said, but I would like to begin with one junior high school since the boys at Maxey work approximately on that level. If the program is successful in one school, then we can transfer it to other schools and other levels. Hansen's group was disappointed, and said so. If it was worth doing, then it was worth doing well (for "well" read "big" in the language of modern education). But if one school was really all I wanted, then I should take Garnet-Patterson Junior High School and set it up properly for the experiment. I agreed. What proper setup had they in mind?

What they had in mind were two radical adjustments. First, the school was overcrowded by almost one in three. An obvious change was to redistribute this extra third amongst other schools. Second, the school had the usual spectrum of quality in its English teachers. Obviously, bad ones must be replaced by good ones from other schools. Was there anything else in the way of student and personnel change I might want? No, I said, I didn't think so. Nor did I think we ought to waste any effort testing the experiment. At the same time that I installed the program I would invent and report experimental results. Which would certainly save a good deal of money, not to mention the anguish of waiting to discover whether the program was a success or a failure.

Educators generally have a short supply of humor. People who do not take testing seriously do not fall anywhere within their notion of what is humorous. Was I suggesting that we not test "English In Every Classroom" in a serious and professional way? Indeed I was, I replied. Why bother with testing when success is guaranteed? What program could fail with class size greatly reduced and bad teachers eliminated? Given good teachers and small classes, even the most witless program would be likely to register measurable success.

My point was considered and taken. I got what I wanted: one junior high school with students and faculty intact. In return I promised to apply for a federal contract to defray my expenses for the next year. Our bargain made, I returned to Michigan with my head full of plans and figures. I thought of many things, but I did not think of the children whose minds and bodies would supply raw data for the experiment. Even had I thought of them, I could not have anticipated Cleo, Wentworth, Snapper, Rubbergut, and Uncle Wiggly.

1

I WAS waiting on the corner across from school. It
was Cleo who brought them to see me. She was in front, with
Wentworth, Snapper, and Rubbergut walking together in the
rear. Because I was sitting, she sat too. Snapper squatted
behind me, Wentworth and Rubbergut leaned against the
telephone pole, while Uncle Wiggly continued to shadowbox
in the street.

"You still wanna know?" she asked.

I told her that I did.

"All right," she said. "Go on, Wentworth. Tell him."

For two days I had hounded him. It began on Thursday
morning when I sat in his English classroom during the first
period of the day. Charles Dickens would have recognized
the teacher. Invented and educated in another age, she was
uncomfortable and unhappy in the seventh decade of the
twentieth century. If silence is golden, her classroom was
the Fort Knox of the neighborhood. Thirty-eight children in
her room that morning, breathing not apparent in thirty-
five. They had long since gotten the message: Keep quiet.
Keep your mouth shut and nothing can happen to you. Say

something, anything, and you've said too much. Thirty-five children sat stifled in silence.

Wentworth sat second seat from the front, second row from the wall. I sat in the last seat of the row next to the wall; the teacher's desk was diagonally across the room from me and at right angles to Wentworth. She had a view of his left side and front while I could see his right side and back. What she saw from the left-front was one more of the silent creatures who inhabited the room like fish displaced from voiceless depths. What I saw from the right-rear was a boy slowly turning the pages of a hot-rod magazine.

The class proceeded through its parody of education, following a formula validated in a thousand classrooms I have visited and countless thousands I have not. First step in the formula is an assumption, an untested hypothesis which becomes valid merely because (and as soon as) it is assumed: Children who do not easily take the imprint of their teacher's own education and values, who are not ductile enough to be drawn wire-thin so that they may slip through traditional holes in the fabric of society—these are not "promising children" and the best that can be hoped for from them is good behavior (silence) and early withdrawal (dropout). Since silence is their most positive attribute, they should be left unmolested during the class hour so long as they practice that virtue.

Perhaps worst of all the many dreadful aspects of this assumption is that *the children know it*. They know—and will tell you, as they told me, if they are asked—that a few of them are regarded as "good material" and the rest are nothing: "Ever' time I go to her class, she make me feel like I was nothin'." Snapper, Rubbergut's half brother, said it. He said it for all the children who drown in the well of silence.

Class of thirty-eight, three being taught. If not being taught, then three volunteering answers. Machines can do it better, and their humanity won't get in the way. Machines can't be hurt by the impersonal voice of the system—a conspiracy of teachers, methods, materials—when it says clearly: "You're dumb. You can't say it right, so don't say it at all." The dumb ones shut up and shut in, but they neither forgive nor forget!

"I just don't understand what those people could be thinking about. I mean, burning down *their own* homes and neighborhoods! I mean, now that's really crazy."

Self-destruction. The only self-expression left to people who don't have anything else to say that anybody will listen to. Of course that's not the whole explanation, and perhaps it's only a small part of it. But it *is*; and insomuch as it is, it's a creature of the schools, a creature bred and fed on the dreadful silences of classrooms for unpromising children.

Wentworth turned pages in his magazine while the teacher and her three right-answer machines dragged the class through its hour burlesque of "English." Most of the students sat in a disembodied trance, staring blindly into the utter emptiness of incoherence. Some drew pictures, others put their heads down on their arms, a few unbroken ones whispered. Halfway through the hour even they had given up, and the only sounds in the classroom were the voices of the teacher and her three performers.

Then it happened—one of those terrible, unmeant confrontations which occur in a classroom whose front corners are filled with the eyes of children avoiding the eyes of the teacher who is equally interested in avoiding theirs. The error was approximately the same on both sides. The teacher meant her question for the girl sitting just east of Wentworth; her glance wasn't off by more than two degrees. Wentworth meant to look west through the windows; at worst, he looked west-southwest. The teacher looked at Wentworth, he looked at her. Neither meant it; both wanted to withdraw, but honor demanded engagement. Helplessly eye-locked, they stared at each other until Wentworth broke the strangled silence by speaking.

What he said doesn't matter. Perhaps he even tried to answer the question—if he heard it, remembered it, understood it. Whatever he said was dreadfully wrong. Without a visitor in class, he might have said nothing. Without a visitor in class, she might have left him to his invisible magazine. As it was, she blushed, he stammered, she upbraided his inattention, and the neighboring machine supplied the answer. Everyone was upset, the visitor included.

When the bell rang, I tried to be first out the door. Knowing that an explanation was coming, I wanted only to avoid it. But the teacher had been trained by years of classroom visitors. Her elapsed time from desk to door was amazing.

"Doctor Fader," she said ("Doctor" is wielded like a club in the public schools); "Doctor Fader, you know what's wrong with that boy? He's so upset and mean and acts so dumb because he's frustrated. He's frustrated because he can't read. I mean, he can't read at all. That makes him feel evil. And then he acts like that. All because he can't read."

She continued to talk but I didn't hear. Can't read? I had just spent forty-five minutes watching him turn the pages of a magazine. Can't read? Can he really have spent all that time looking at pictures? Because I had to believe my eyes, I couldn't believe my ears. Who can give that kind of attention to printed page after printed page—no matter what the quality of the illustrations—and not be able to read? Certainly not an upset, dumb, evil kid.

Another piece of evidence awaited me when I walked into the corridor. Wentworth was lounging against his locker, talking to a group of boys whom I later came to know as members of Cleo's gang. Because he was absorbed in his friends and because the corridor was full of sound and movement, I was able to examine his face without warning him to close it upon pain of discovery.

In our assessment of children's intellect, we have consistently failed to take advantage of a reliable sign. Who has not remarked the bright eyes that are one sure signal of engagable children? "He's trouble. You can see it in his eyes." And "She just *looks* intelligent." These are different facets of the same jewel, though we are often fools enough to think one precious and the other worthless. The child whose life still lights his eyes—in spite of our judgment of proper illumination—is the only "promising" child. Because he still hopes for himself, we dare not do less. Wentworth, mean and upset and frustrated as he may have been, had as bright a pair of eyes as ever planned trouble in a school corridor.

For all that remained of Thursday and again on Friday I followed him from class to class. By Friday noon I had seen enough; we spoke in the cafeteria:

"She says you can't read. I don't believe it."

"Maybe she jus' puttin' you on."

"Maybe you're just putting her on." We had a talking acquaintance, no more. I knew I might be presuming too much, might be invading the place where the boy kept himself hidden, but the week was nearly done and I knew I was close to the truth I had begun to suspect. When he said, in a flat voice, "I ain't doin' nothin' to nobody," my impatience and irritation must have shown in my face, for suddenly he turned away from me—we had been standing together in the cafeteria line—and took a place farther back, his face averted.

I ate quickly at a table with several teachers and waited for Wentworth to finish. I knew I wouldn't get anything from him that he didn't want to give, and I thought he would be least likely to feel like giving when he was in the company of friends. As in so many of my estimates of children, I was wrong about the effect of his friends upon Wentworth. But I erred even more than habitual underestimation can explain. I was so wrong because Cleo was completely beyond my experience.

After I had eaten quickly, wanting to be ready whenever Wentworth decided to leave, I found myself feeling like a fool as both teachers and children, who had eaten at a more sensible rate, finished their meals and their conversations and left the cafeteria. No one had left Wentworth's table by the time the last teacher departed from mine. As the only adult remaining in the room, I suddenly felt conspicuous and alone.

When the last teacher left the cafeteria, five expressionless children got up together and walked toward me across the room. As they slowly made their way through the tables, I realized that I was not only conspicuous and alone, I was also uneasy and apprehensive. Had I harassed Wentworth to the point that he had enlisted his friends to help him handle me? I pushed my chair back from the table and stood up to meet them. The cafeteria was empty but for the six of us. They formed a semicircle in the aisle while I faced them from between the tables.

"Why you messin' on Wentworth?" The only girl in the group was speaking to me. No preliminaries. Just the question.

"I'm not messing on anybody," I said.

"Shi-i." It was Wentworth, commenting on the truth of my answer. The girl ignored him and watched me.

"He don't wanna talk to you," she said.

"But I want to talk to him. He could help me a lot if he wanted to."

"He don't want to."

"He should."

"Why he *should*?" She was surprised and turned to look at Wentworth to see if there was something he hadn't told her. A gesture of his shoulders was enough. She turned her attention to me.

"What were you looking at during your English class yesterday and today?" I asked Wentworth.

"Nothin'."

"Shi-i," I said, imitating his response to my untruthful answer. The girl laughed loudly. The others grinned, their attention on Wentworth and not on me.

"Lookin' at a hogbook," he said slowly, a smile lighting his face as he realized what I had said and who I was imitating.

"Which one?"

"Don't know the name."

"*Hot Rod?*"

" 'At the one."

"You like it?"

"Some."

"Where'd you get it from?"

"Teacher had a pile of 'em onna table."

"You know where *she* got it from?" An eloquent movement of his shoulders and eyes. "I gave it to her," I said.

"You the one brung all them newspapers and magazines?" The girl was interested. So were the others.

"Yes. Friends give them to me and I bring them to you." It was hard to find the right tone. Who was I speaking to? Children? Adults who looked like children? I needed them for what they could tell me, especially Wentworth. But I didn't seem to be getting any closer to the information I wanted.

"So Wentworth oughta talk to you on accoun' of he was lookin' at a magazine you brung?" Skepticism was in her voice.

"No," I said, realizing that was exactly what I had meant.

"He ought to talk to me because he knows a lot of things I need to know."

"Like what?" she asked, disbelief spreading from her voice to her face. "Like what?" she said again, more loudly, as the bell rang for change of class.

I was helpless. The whole thing was in her hands now, this girl with her retinue of grinning, disbelieving boys. Mine may not be the oldest profession, I thought, but it has to be the worst. Who else has to depend on the whims of children? I had already given up hope when I answered her: "Like why his teachers say he can't read and I see him reading a hog-book for two days in his English class?"

It was all unreal. Standing in the cafeteria of the Garnet-Patterson Junior High School on Tenth between U and V streets in northwest Washington, negotiating with a barely adolescent girl for information from a barely adolescent boy. In less than six hours I would board an airplane and fly back to my own world in Ann Arbor. I was beginning to think I should never have left it.

The bell rang again and the girl spoke: "We gotta go now. After school we meets on the corner 'cross from the front door." She turned and led them out of the cafeteria. None of them even glanced back at me as they left.

2

BEFORE GOING to meet them I went to see one of their teachers. A big, bluff man, he had meant to befriend me earlier in the autumn by calling several of his fellow teachers liars when one of them told me, in our weekly Thursday afternoon meeting, that they were making full use of 450 daily copies of *The Washington Post* I had obtained as a gift from the newspaper's publisher.

"There's mighty little truth in that. No sir!" he had announced from the back of the room when one of the English teachers was reporting on the school's use of the newspaper. She had tried to ignore him and finish her report, but he wouldn't be ignored. "Maybe you doing what you say," he said to her when she paused for breath, "but I *know* a whole lot of people not using them papers *at all*."

I knew it, too, but thought I had everything to lose by saying so, and was afraid I'd lose as much if anybody else said so. Nonuse of new materials was a problem I had expected; given time enough, I believed it could be solved. This man was giving me no time.

"Me and my boys collects those papers every day, and *we*

know who uses 'em and who don't. Can't use a newspaper without mussing it up some. No sir!"

Who can ever be certain of what will move people to action? My friend provoked more newspaper usage with a thirty-second speech from the back of the room than I had been able to accomplish with hours of speeches from the front. As he told me with vast satisfaction several weeks after the incident, "I can't swear they being used, but they sure being mussed up!"

Now I needed some information and he was my most reliable source. No sooner had I described the girl and mentioned Wentworth's name—the only one I knew—when he turned away and stared out the window. But I had time to see his normally affable face become troubled before it turned from my view. When he swung back to me, he was somebody else:

"You don't want to mess with them," he said.

"Are they dangerous?" I remembered my feeling as they came toward me across the cafeteria.

"Them? Shoot. . . ." He waved away what I had said. I hadn't understood, but he had said nothing for me to understand. I waited while he continued to stare out the window. As usual I felt I was playing a game without knowing the rules. I was tired of being an alien; I got up to go.

"Hey!" he said, real surprise on his face, "I haven't told you *nothing*."

"Don't I know it," I answered. "And that's all you're planning to tell me. What should I wait for?"

"Hold on now. Hold on." He was visibly upset by my irritation but he still hadn't made up his mind. "You couldn't just leave 'em be?"

"I can leave the whole thing be."

But I couldn't, and neither could he. Finally he told me. He couldn't tell it quickly and he didn't tell it easily. For the first time he talked to me about color—how he didn't know whether a white man could understand about a colored girl like Cleo; how he didn't want me to think that she and her boys were like other children in the school, but they weren't so different either; how they worried him because he didn't know what to do about them, so he did nothing. Could I understand about a fourteen-year-old girl who led a gang of boys, who formed her gang and kept it together by letting them lay her on a regular schedule? No, he said, looking away again, he didn't think I could understand about that.

We left it there while he told me what he knew about the five of them: Her name was Cleo and I already knew Wentworth. The littlest one was called Uncle Wiggly because he was always twitching and moving and dancing, and the other two were Snapper and Rubbergut who were half brothers. All except Rubbergut were at least a cut above the other kids in the school when it came to brains; Rubbergut's membership in the group was probably due to his being Snapper's brother. Snapper was quick and sudden, Wentworth was sure, and Cleo was more of everything than both of them put together.

How did he know so much about them? One of the boys had talked to him and never mind which one. But if I was going to have something to do with them, I had to accept that Cleo was their real leader. Not just because she had what they wanted, but because she was smarter and tougher than any of them. Wentworth was the only one in the gang who could stand up to her if he had to.

We both had to be elsewhere. I was grateful and I told him so. He turned from me in the corridor, then turned again and poked a finger into my arm as he said: "You get them on your side. They be a real help to you around here."

3

WENTWORTH TOLD ME. "Sure I can read," he said. "I been able to read ever since I can remember. But I ain't never gonna let *them* know, on accoun' of iff'n I do I'm gonna have to read all that crap they got."

I knew what he said was true. I knew it was true because I had seen him reading; I knew it was true because I'd seen the brightness in his eyes and heard the deft quickness of his responses. I had assumed such children existed when I first conceived the approach to teaching literacy that was slowly making its way from Michigan to the District of Columbia. But though I knew it was true with every sense and instinct I had, I could barely believe what I had heard. A theory is a disembodied thing. To watch a theory take arms and legs and tongue. . . . I realized that they were all waiting for me to speak.

"You know who Albert Einstein is?" I asked.

"Sure," said Cleo. "He was a dumbhead when he was a kid. Then he done all kind a smart things. I read 'bout him in a magazine."

My question had been pure rhetoric. They must get mighty

tired of being underestimated, I thought. Tired enough to pretend they're too stupid to read. "You know what," I said, "I didn't think you'd know who he was. I'm sorry."

"Don't matter. How come you wanna know?"

"Because when Wentworth told me he really can read even though everybody thinks he can't, I guess I felt like Einstein after astronomers proved he was right when he said there had to be a planet like Neptune. He must have felt pretty good, and so do I."

"Just 'cause Wentworth can read?"

"Just because I've always been sure there must be a lot of people like Wentworth but I never met one before. It's worth a lot to me to know I'm right."

"How much?"

"How much what?"

"How much it worth to know you right?"

"I'll have to think about it some. You got a suggestion?"

"Anyway a dollar."

"Anyway," I said. "How about a dollar and a quarter? That comes out to...."

"I know what it come to. A dollar and twenty-five is a quarter for ever' one of us. You can give it to us now if you wants to."

I counted the money out and she put it in the pocket of her coat. Thinking the interview was done, I got up from the curb to go to my car parked across the street.

"Don't you wanna hear Wentworth read somethin'?"

"Should I?" I was too surprised to find the right response.

"He could fool his teachers, he could fool you."

She was right. He could, and so could she if she wanted to. Maybe they all could. I sat down again while Wentworth opened the paperbound book that Snapper was carrying. It was Joy Adamson's *Born Free*, the story of Elsa the lioness who grows up as a member of the Adamson family. Wentworth chose to read the passage that describes Elsa's first meeting with an elephant:

> It was an exciting moment when the cub met her first elephant, an anxious one too, for poor Elsa had no mother to warn her against those animals who regard lions as the only enemies of their young and therefore sometimes kill them. . . .

As he read, I managed to look at their faces. Rubbergut's mouth was open; Uncle Wiggly was momentarily in repose. He had their rapt attention. I was sure that all I had to do was close my eyes and I'd find myself walking through the looking glass or down the yellow-brick road—nothing I could imagine would be less likely than sitting on a street corner in northwest Washington while an illiterate boy read *Born Free* to me and the other members of his gang.

"O.K.?" It was Cleo, and she was speaking to me.

"Sure. Fine. I'm satisfied."

"You bring the books, too?"

"Yes. From a friend of mine."

"He some friend." It was Snapper, breaking his silence for the first time.

"He is. Would you like to meet him sometime and see all the books he has?"

"Sometime." The meeting was finished. Cleo had spoken the last word with a finality that none of us could miss. I watched them walk down the street in a close group. Again, none looked back.

4

FOR THE FIRST TIME in three months I was looking forward to returning to Washington. At the end of August and early in September, when I had begun to visit the school each Thursday and Friday and meet with faculty on a weekly basis, I had been sustained by my own enthusiasm and its reflection in the principal and some of his teachers. Caught up by the strength of my belief in an approach that had worked so well in the improbable environment of a prison school, the few who joined me immediately began to recruit a growing number of colleagues to the program. Then the growth stopped, abruptly and almost completely. I was hard up against the absolute intransigence of the incompetent but tenured teacher.

The weekly Thursday afternoon meetings brought full measure of anger and frustration to everyone. By the end of November, just before Thanksgiving, I was almost ready to join the principal in forcing the worst of his teachers to request assignment to another school for the second semester. The idea was attractive because it was easily implemented: The Superintendent had repeated his offer to improve the faculty in order to give my program a better chance of success. Attractive though the idea was, it would be—if implemented—a flat admission of failure. Public school curricula are full of programs that work under "special circumstances," i.e., conditions unobtainable in the average school system. If my program became one more in the category of levers too short to be used by the normally weak, if it required abnormal strength of teaching in order to obtain purchase in the world of learning, then it was worthless and a fraud. By the end of November, fraudulence was beginning to seem a minor crime.

The Thanksgiving holiday put two weeks between visits and helped me to recover both hope and perspective. Wentworth's admission and performance were treatment and tonic, for his very existence had been denied by teachers throughout the United States. I first began to suspect his presence when my research into the nature and nurture of literacy led me to ask reading specialists and English teachers to estimate the percentage of functional illiterates we could expect in children remanded to prison school. Their answer, between two-thirds and three-quarters, astounded me. Two-thirds of 600 children is an impossible number. What small, state-supported school would ever have enough money and space to hire, house, and equip specialists necessary to remediate reading distempers and diseases of 400 illiterate children? Not we, not ever. If the figure were only partly accurate, our task was beyond our strength.

I asked for explanations. What could possibly account for such a high percentage of illiteracy? Whose fault and what remedy? The answers had a remarkable unanimity: Blame must be placed where it properly belongs—on teachers and methods in the first three grades. So many children were confused and alienated by the time they entered fourth grade that only miracles of effort and attention could reclaim them. If one wanted to unwind the tangled skein of illiteracy, especially illiteracy of impoverished children, one had to begin in the first three grades. . . .

I listened to these accusations, repeated in substance by school people from all sections of the country, and I observed that none of those who placed the fault in the shifting strata of three primary grades was or had been a teacher in those grades. Having observed this, I was reminded of the defense of ineffective freshman English courses I have heard offered by colleagues in colleges and universities: What, after all, can we hope to accomplish in a brief year when we are given students so badly prepared by their high school English teachers? First three grades; last three grades—the practice of assigning responsibility for a child's failure, whether absolute or comparative, to some dimly seen figure in the lightless past, is as reprehensible in reading specialists as it is in English professors. In neither case does it help the student.

Because I had seldom found collegiate charges against high school English teachers to be substantial, I was skeptical of similar charges against teachers in the first three grades. My skepticism, however, was based on more than analogy: Having accepted responsibility for designing a language program for illiterate delinquents, I felt obliged to revisit the imputed source of illiteracy. Much to my surprise I discovered that no radical alterations had taken place in species or genus of primary school teachers in the quarter-century since last I had known them. They were still women and they were still maternal, especially in the first three grades.

Both qualifications are significant. Each supplies a condition important to the nurture of literacy in the primary grades. Though a few men teach in grades one through three, their number is minute. Women are the body and spirit of early school experience for children, and most children regard them as mother-substitutes. Teachers so regarded must nevertheless earn their student's affection. No young child can be deceived for very long about how an adult—especially an exposed adult—feels about him. Since long-term deception is impossible to the naked adults who are teachers, the first and last requirement upon teachers of young children is that they like their students. This is a unique requirement of the early grades. Beyond the third or fourth grade, children are generally too wise to make such a demand upon their teachers.

All this by way of saying that a great proportion of teachers in the first three grades are maternal women who like children and children know it. Only individual teachers have changed in the past quarter-century; the kind remains the same. Equally, children remain unchanged in their most significant relationship to school: They are, in grades where reading is taught, still anxious to learn.

Combine the nature of teachers with the readiness of children, and mass illiteracy at the end of third grade seems unlikely *no matter how reading is taught in the schools*. This does not imply that all methods are of like value nor that all children learn to read before they enter the fourth grade. What is clear to me, however, is that bad teaching in the first three grades is not the primary cause of apparent illiteracy in adolescents, and that most children learn to read reasonably early in their school careers.

How then to account for the enormous number of functional illiterates who inhabit schools from fourth grade until the age of merciful release? First, a definition: I use the phrase "functional illiterate" to describe the person, whether child or adult, who has had enough reading instruction to support the supposition that he could have learned to read. This makes him very different from the true illiterate who has had either no instruction or so little that no one can reasonably expect him to be able to read. The functional illiterate may be able to read; he simply cannot or *will not* read well enough for written language to bring him either profit or pleasure.

The emphasis of this last statement reveals my own belief: Having heard accusatory accounts of reading instruction in the early grades; having assessed that instruction and found it inaccurately portrayed, though needing much to make it good; having seen for myself fearful numbers of apparent illiterates inhabiting school classrooms beyond third or fourth grade—I therefore assumed the existence of a child born human who had been re-created a monster by the schools. I assumed the existence of a growing tribe of Wentworths, children who cautiously entered the house called literacy—even if by the back door—and discovered floors awry, mirrors crazed, and furniture built to serve other creatures. Recognizing a hostile environment, they retreated through doors and windows and had been retreating ever since.

What is more monstrous than the creature that learns to deny its own existence? Make that creature a child like Wentworth who learns to hide, for self-protection, the intellect that is one distinguishing mark of his humanity, and the making of a monstrosity becomes the creation of a tragedy. Though I grieved for Wentworth, I searched for him and rejoiced to find him. He was the first child I had found, identified by his teachers as a functional illiterate, who could in fact read with ease.

Proof of Wentworth's existence confirmed the most radical assumption of my program for teaching literacy. That assumption imputed latent, functional literacy to the vast majority of adolescents identified by their previous school performance as functional illiterates. Its importance was paramount to our efforts, for its most powerful implication is that adolescent illiteracy in the schools is *more apparent than real*, that children could and would remediate themselves if reading were made so pervasive in the curriculum that they could not deny it, and so pleasurable in the classroom that they would not wish to avoid it.

As I write this, seven years after making the assumption and two years after publishing the statistical and anecdotal proof of its validity (*Hooked on Books*, 1968), I remember my uncertainty as I prepared newly hired teachers in an unopened penal school to use methods and materials designed for children who wouldn't read rather than children who couldn't read. Fifteen months after that long August of seminars, arguments, visions, and revisions, I sat on a streetcorner in Washington and listened to Wentworth read from the best-selling paperback story of a lioness raised by humans in the semiarid thornbush of Kenya. At the time, raising that lioness in Africa seemed no more unlikely than listening to that boy in America.

5

WHEN I RETURNED to Garnet-Patterson on the
Thursday after Thanksgiving, I returned accompanied by a
problem. The problem was a black Cadillac which Hertz
gave me in place of the Ford I usually rented at the airport.
On this particular Thursday they had no record of my reservation and no other car. Avis and National had no cars at all
except by reservation, and I had to have a car to keep appointments at the U.S. Office of Education and the
Superintendent's office on Thursday morning, as well as
with a group of librarians in Baltimore on Friday afternoon.
I took the Cadillac but I wasn't happy. Neither the neighborhood nor the situation made me feel comfortable about
being a white man in a Cadillac.

With my special parking permit, the car sat on Tenth
Street in front of school all afternoon. Even though I had a
meeting with faculty immediately after school, I was leaning against the car when the kids came out. Since at least a
quarter of the faculty had found some way to mention the
car to me during and after lunch, I was sure the children
must know about it too. I had seen Cleo and each member
of her gang in various classes, and I had seen them together
in the cafeteria, but I had merely nodded my head in recog-

nition. I wanted them to come to me—I had already made the invitation—and I thought the car might be a magnet strong enough to draw them.

It was. Cleo was nothing if not direct: "That bomb really somethin'," she said to me as she led her boys slowly past it on the sidewalk. Others were watching, and I realized that even for Cleo both prestige and self-esteem were involved in being connected with that Cadillac.

"It's big," I said, as blandly as possible.

"How come you drivin' it?" asked Snapper. "You ain't never driven nothin' but Fords before."

"New Fords," corrected Wentworth.

"Different one ever' time," said Uncle Wiggly. It was the first time I had heard him speak.

"They don't belong to me," I said. "I rent them. All I could get this time was a Cadillac."

"Tough," said Snapper. They all laughed.

"It go pretty good?" asked Wentworth.

"Pretty good."

"Do a hunnert?" asked Uncle Wiggly.

"I guess," I said. "No place to do a hundred around here."

"Sure is," he replied. "Do a hunnert onna beltway iff'n the cops ain't lookin'."

"Yeah," said Wentworth. "And if they lookin', you ass belong to them."

Wentworth and Uncle Wiggly were talking while Cleo was making up her mind. "You going our way?" She had decided for all of them.

"Not now," I said. "I've got a meeting with the teachers. If you're here at 4:30, I'll be going your way."

"We be here."

I had been concerned for the car's safety after school, for some of the teachers' cars had been vandalized during the autumn after the children had been dismissed for the day. If a kid was feeling destructive, the Cadillac was a natural target. As I reentered the school I realized I had nothing to worry about. No more devoted guards were available at any price.

When the meeting was done, I left quickly before anyone could engage me in conversation. Within the school nothing had changed in two weeks and I had been a fool to think it would. If anything, positions had hardened. Of fifty-odd teachers in the faculty, perhaps fifteen were working at translating principles of "English In Every Classroom" into classroom practices. They had given up old methods and materials to use newspapers, magazines, and paperbound books as their daily texts, and to use teaching methods we had developed in the penal school. The converts were zealous, but the heathen fought for old gods: "I am not trained to be an English teacher and I will not teach English." A ponderous woman said that, ponderously, during the meeting. Ten heads nodded in agreement. Perhaps another ten would have liked to.

I knew what was needed, but I didn't know where to find it. What I wanted was strength beyond any persuasion that principal, partisans, and I could bring to bear, but strength less than the coercion available to the Superintendent. I still wanted teachers who would cooperate unwillingly, and I would put up with some who wouldn't cooperate at all. The uncommitted twenty-five were the ones I was fighting for; but at the battle's present forward pace, the school year would be completed before I had won their help. Depressed at results of the meeting, I retreated to Cleo, her boys, and the Cadillac.

All except Uncle Wiggly were waiting by the car. "He be right back," Cleo told me. "He always fidgetin' and he got to pee a lot." She could have been his mother instead of his mistress. She could have been his mother *and* his mistress. She could have been anything at all. Uncle Wiggly came at full speed around the corner.

"Let's go," Snapper said. "I ain't got no more waitin' time."

"You've been waiting too long for only a ride home," I said. "How about going down along the river just to see if she can make it."

"She make it," said Wentworth softly as he patted the hood. "She make it alright."

Cleo and Wentworth sat up front with me; Snapper, Rubbergut, and Uncle Wiggly sat in the rear. There was a brief struggle for windows, a struggle which Cleo settled by assigning Rubbergut to the middle seat. We drove slowly through the neighborhood, three of our four windows down even though it was a cold first week in December, before we turned south on Fourteenth Street to find the Potomac. Nobody said a word as they put the windows up and settled back into leather upholstery. I knew how they felt. I could remember the first time I had ridden in a Cadillac.

As we crossed Fourteenth Street bridge, a four-engine propeller plane soared up in front of us into the late afternoon sky. "Listen," I said, "I don't want to drive this car to Baltimore tomorrow if I don't have to. If you've got time, I'll stop at the airport and see if Hertz can rent me another."

"We got time," said Cleo.

"All kindsa time." It was Uncle Wiggly, leaning forward in the seat behind me.

"How come you don' wanna wheel this bomb to Baltimore?" Wentworth was astounded. He was staring at me across Cleo's profile.

"For every dollar I spend to rent a Ford, I have to put out a dollar and a half for a Cadillac. The trip to Baltimore would eat me up."

"My teacher say the gov'min payin' for you." Rubbergut, unexpectedly.

"Shoot. What *you* know about it?" Snapper, with enormous disdain.

"Your teacher's right. What she didn't say was that the

money I've got has to last the whole year. When it's gone, it's gone."

"Gov'min got plenty more."

"Sure. But not for me."

"Seem like a shame not to keep this'n." Wentworth was unreconciled to the loss.

We were nearing a peak time for air traffic. The sky seemed full of planes as we approached the airport. I drove as slowly as I could to let them watch the takeoffs.

"You been on one a them?" Rubbergut was leaning as far across Uncle Wiggly as he dared in order to see the planes through the window.

"Sure he been on one a them! Man, you *so* dumb. How you think he get here ever' week?" Snapper had no mercy. I watched Rubbergut's face in the mirror. He looked as though he had long ago tuned his brother out.

"It's the best way for me to get here," I said. "Takes about three hours from my house to your school. If I didn't fly, it would take maybe twelve hours in a car."

"Drive *this'n*," said Wentworth, "and I bet you get here pretty near as fast as any ole airplane."

"You know how far it is from my house to your school?" I asked.

"Mor'n a hunnert miles," answered Cleo decisively.

I abandoned the topics of speed and distance. Even television isn't powerful enough to convince a child whose life is tightly bound by street intersections and leg power that speeds and distances beyond the magic figure of 100 are real. A whole concept of number that we extrapolate from our own experience and teach in school is utterly meaningless to impoverished children. We are worse than irrelevant; we are incoherent in the eyes and ears of children whose quantitative experience is totally unlike our own.

"How much it cost to buy one a these?" Wentworth was rubbing his hand slowly and gently on wood paneling. His question wasn't really meant for me or for anyone except himself. I wouldn't have answered if he hadn't turned his face toward me and repeated it.

"Maybe seven thousand dollars."

When no reaction came from anyone in the car I realized that $7,000 was like thousand-mile distances and 600-mile-an-hour speeds. I could just as well have said $17,000 for all the reaction they would have shown. If Mr. Jones buys a house for $40,000 and has twenty years to pay it off, how many apples will each of his ten children get when he goes to the poorhouse? We parked in the circle in front of Washington National Airport.

None of them had ever been there before. When I was in junior high school, growing up in Baltimore, my father would take our ancient car out on a fine Sunday and we would all drive fifty miles to this same airport where we would sit comfortably for the afternoon reading the Sunday paper and watching airplanes. It was a great adventure for us. For them, their homes within five miles of the airport, the adventure was much greater.

I left them sitting in five chairs facing glass windows which make up one wall of the old terminal. When I got to the Hertz desk I kept on going. Dollar-and-a-half for every dollar be damned; I couldn't turn in that Cadillac when a few dollars could purchase so much pleasure for five children. I hid myself in a telephone booth and pretended to be waiting for a call. After ten minutes I returned to the glass wall.

A white policeman had them on their feet and was taking their names. "What's the trouble, officer?" I asked.

"These kids with you?"

"That's right. Why are you taking their names?"

"Because they don't belong here, that's why."

"Were they making a disturbance?"

"We wasn't doing nothing but sitting." Cleo said it flatly, her face turned toward the windows.

"Then why are you bothering them?" I knew why and so did they. I was so angry I had to speak slowly to keep my voice from shaking.

For the first time he looked directly at me. What would have happened had he not seen a well-dressed, very angry white man? "Just checking," he said, closing his notebook and turning away in the same movement. There was no more for anybody to say. We walked slowly back to the car.

"You was ready and he know it," Snapper said as we walked across the parking circle.

"He my man," said Wentworth softly. I heard him clearly, but for a brief moment I didn't know that he was talking about me. Then I understood—they had never before seen anybody who wasn't drunk or crazy stand up to police harrassment. When the badge came around, the best thing you could do was slide. Even if you were guiltless as a suckling babe.

It was Uncle Wiggly who said it first: "Ain't we goin' right back to where we was parked?"

So I told them that Hertz had said it was this one or walk, and Baltimore would be too much for my shoes. But if they were tired of this old Cad, maybe we could take a taxi.

"Aw, no, man, I *likes* this one." Poor Rubbergut. Cleo and Wentworth grinned, Snapper groaned, and we all arranged ourselves again on the leather cushions. We sat for a moment, glad to be back in the car.

"Wentworth say you our man." Cleo looked around at the three in the back seat, then back at me: "You want somethin', it don't cost you nothin'." As we drove out of the airport I thought that tomorrow was Friday and what I wanted was some sort of miraculous help in my battle with the Garnet-Patterson faculty.

6

I HAD FORGOTTEN that Friday was a half-day. Had I remembered, I would have made other arrangements for the afternoon. As it was, I didn't have to be in Baltimore until four o'clock and school was dismissed at noon. By the time I reached the front door, all children and most teachers had gone for the weekend. All children, that is, except Cleo and her gang.

"We got time to go see them books." Cleo, as usual without preliminaries.

"We could just go for a ride." In spite of what had happened yesterday and the way they felt about it, I didn't want them to think they had to go anywhere.

"Could. Can't see them books on Friday?"

"Sure can. If you don't mind riding in a Cad."

The District News Company is located on Bladensburg Road in Cottage City, Maryland, just across the District line. Its founder and active president, Joseph Ottenstein, has built his business from a street corner to a market corner. District News is sole distributor (wholesaler) for paperbound books and magazines in the Greater District area, a territory which extends halfway up Baltimore Pike. Because it handles books and magazines from all publishers, District News is the natural place to go for all popular paperbound publications. With a letter of introduction from Ivan Ludington, the Detroit distributor whose remarkable charity made the Michigan experiment possible, I went to Cottage City to meet Joseph Ottenstein early in September.

Many people with means lack will to help those less fortunate or less happy than themselves. To deplore inequities of life in contemporary America is very stylish and, apparently, very satisfying, for it serves in place of action for so many. Joe Ottenstein was angry at District schools and greatly compassionate for its children. But his anger and compassion did not limit themselves to words. Having the will to put his means to work in righting inequities, and having the habit of doing so, he was doubly frustrated:

"You should see what those teachers choose," he told me. "They come in with their federal grants and choose the same books they've been ordering for years. The same books the kids haven't been reading for years. Only difference now is that they're paperback and its federal money."

In order to change *Silas Marner* into *Black Like Me* he was willing to do more than he had done. He was willing, for instance, to make paperbound books available to Garnet-Patterson at wholesale cost, and to make magazines available for nothing. I didn't think that would be necessary, I told him, though it was certainly generous. What I would appreciate was a supply of materials at maximum educational discount. A lesser price would be too likely to make the experiment unique at the junior high school; other schools, not fortunate enough to have available the generosity of District News, would be unable to duplicate its conditions.

I opened an account in Garnet-Patterson's name. Part of

my agreement with the Superintendent was that he would supply funds, within specified limits, for a portion of materials necessary to the project, while the U.S. Office of Education bore the cost of my services and certain other materials. When I opened the account with District News in September, I had no idea that the company would be asked to supply some materials on faith and the rest on charity until spring of next year.

As we drove out New York Avenue to Bladensburg Road, I told them what Joe Ottenstein had done and was doing for their school. In spite of good intentions, the Superintendent found himself at the mercy of a House committee dominated by Southern congressmen who took their small pleasures in delaying funds for a school district more than ninety percent black. And I was still waiting for final notification of contract approval from the Office of Education, even though that office had originally solicited transfer of my program into a public school setting. Which meant, I said, that Mr. Ottenstein was the man responsible for magazines and paperbound books beginning to appear in school.

"He a Jew?" The question was Cleo's.

"Yes."

"Don't mess none with him. He screw you iff'n he can."

I let it go. Joe Ottenstein is a living argument against anti-Semitism. What Cleo had said, and some of the others had agreed to, was the result of personal experience with a few shopkeepers and landlords. The place to begin a counterattack on that kind of prejudice is also with personal experience—with a man like Joe Ottenstein. The arguments could come later.

We parked beside Ottenstein's Cadillac, a duplicate of the car we were driving. "That a real Jew car," said Cleo.

"Yeah," said Wentworth. "And this a real nigger car." He didn't turn his head from the window, but everybody in the car knew what an enormity had been committed. That was no word to use in front of me. Cleo recognized it for what it was, a direct challenge to her words and her beliefs; there was a mighty silence in the car.

"That ain't no kinda name to put on this car." Cleo had taken a long time to reply. Her tone was as mild as her words.

"O.K." said Wentworth. "Then *that* a real nigger car." He opened the door and got out. Snapper and Uncle Wiggly did the same from the back seat. The rest of us followed more slowly. I had a lot more invested in this visit to District News than I had intended. And Joe Ottenstein didn't even know we were coming.

An hour and a half later we returned to the car. The kids were dazed, and with good reason, for Ottenstein's reception had been dazzling. It was a performance possible only to a rich seventy-year-old man who can see the world through the eyes of poor adolescent children. Even now, four years after the fact, it's difficult to write objectively about that visit.

We began in Ottenstein's handsome office and we ended there. In between was a laying on of gifts—paperbound books, magazines—that seemed to have no end. Halfway through the building it was necessary to find cartons for everybody. Uncle Wiggly, much the smallest, was already disappearing beneath his load. Before the cartons came, I had the powerful desire to take a picture of Wentworth, both hands full of paperbound books, and leave it without comment on his English teacher's desk. Seldom can a functional illiterate have functioned so efficiently in a house of literacy.

Notes I made after that visit are mostly sentimental or personal or both. What seems now to bear retelling are several incidents that took place during our tour of the premises:

Joe Ottenstein's habit is to make a present of books to his

visitors. To adults he gives copies of books he has read himself. Reading constantly, moving from office to car to home
and a hundred other places, he has developed a habit which
effectively assures him that no one will remove the paperback book he is reading: Each time he is interrupted, each
time he lays the book down—he tears out pages he has read.

Lying on the table in his office was a book missing its
cover and first eighty pages. A more incongruous article in
that office in that building is difficult to imagine. I knew
every one saw it, and I knew I'd hear about it. The first time
our host left us to greet a visitor, we were still in his office.
No sooner had he left the room than Snapper asked for all
of them, "Who tear up that book?"

"Mr. Ottenstein," I said. "It's one he's reading."

"How you know?"

"Because the cover and some pages are missing."

"Why he do that?"

"Gives him strength."

"What?" Ten eyes shuttled from the book to me.

"That's right," I said. "He eats 'em."

"Sure," said Wentworth. "Sure he do."

"He has all his books printed on special sweet paper," I
said. "Then he doesn't have to get up for a snack when he's
reading. All he has to do is rip off a few pages and chew 'em
up."

They were stretched taut. The confrontation between Cleo
and Wentworth had only served to tighten their already
tense, ambiguous feelings about where they were going and
what they were going to do. If I couldn't get them to relax,
the visit would be unpleasant for everybody.

"How come he don't have some honey or strawber' jam on
'em?" Cleo was the first to pick me up.

"Shoot," said Snapper, a big smile spreading over his face,
"couldn't do that on accoun' the pages be sticky."

THE NAKED CHILDREN   43

Wentworth and Uncle Wiggly grinned at the same time. Uncle Wiggly leaned toward the desk and picked up another paperbound with a dark brown cover: "Who wants a couple pages a chocolate?"

"Watch yourself, boy," Wentworth warned him. "That ain't chocolate; that Ex-Lax."

The four of them collapsed with laughter. Even Rubbergut guffawed. It had all been deep for him, but he understood the humor in confusing chocolate with Ex-Lax.

They were themselves as we toured the building. I was surprised at their very different reactions to magazines and to books. The tour began at the bottom of the building, on the floor where magazines are handled. To my eyes, there's more motion, color, and excitement in sorting and shipping magazines than in the rest of the business together; but my eyes are not theirs. They were attentive, they were interested in the baling machine, they were highly pleased to be given their unlimited choice of magazines—but they seemed somehow to have imagined all this before, and their reaction was quiet and familiar.

The magazines may only have warmed them, but the books kindled them to a flame. They could barely contain themselves: "*All* them books," breathed Wentworth. "All them motherin' books!"

Row after row after row. . . . Before being called away for the last time, having already made boxes necessary by the quantity of his gifts, Mr. Ottenstein told me to let them take whatever paperbacks they wanted. "As many as they can carry," he said as he left the floor. The kids heard, but we were all reluctant to select anything without him to help us. Then an employee came to find us amongst the rows. Mr. Ottenstein had some work he couldn't postpone; he'd meet us in his office when we were on our way out.

It was a combination of Rubbergut and Edgar Rice Bur-

roughs that broke the children's reserve. Burroughs not only
wrote two dozen books with Tarzan as hero, he was also
guilty of an equal number of science fiction novels. District
News had most of both kinds, published between paper covers by Ace and Ballantine, all shelved together in their endless stacks. When we noticed Rubbergut was missing, we
backtracked through the rows until we found him slowly
filling his box with a copy of every one of forty-odd Burroughs books the company had in stock. He asked us to come
and get him when we were done. If it was alright, he was
just gonna sit right there and start reading one a them
books.

We lost Uncle Wiggly to the Peanuts books, and Snapper
to James Bond. Since both Cleo and Wentworth wanted to
fill up on race books, which at the time were not shelved
together, the three of us made our way through most of the
company's inventory. A year earlier, before my experience
with children in a Michigan prison school, I would have been
incredulous at their knowledge. While we were being guided
by Mr. Ottenstein, they had been cataloguing books they
really wanted. They both knew about Richard Wright and
James Baldwin and each took a copy of every one of their
books on the shelves. No, they didn't know about Martin
Duberman and Essien-Udom and John Howard Griffin, but
Dick Gregory was Wentworth's man and Cleo knew all there
was to know about Althea Gibson. She had read *I Always
Wanted to Be Somebody* twice but she took it anyway. She'd
think of somebody to give it to.

Wentworth took Gallagher and Colvin's *Words Most Often
Misspelled and Mispronounced* without saying anything
about it. Both took a copy of Harry Golden's book, *Mr. Ken-
nedy and the Negroes*. I found something else to look at
when Cleo picked up Alan Guttmacher's *Pregnancy and
Birth*. Seeing her looking at it thoughtfully made me too
much aware of what my friend had told me about her and

her boys. What could I do about it? It was none of my business. Even so, it made me uncomfortable.

Both took *South Town* and *Raisin in the Sun*, but only Wentworth was interested in Arnold Hano's *Willie Mays*. Each took all three of Chester Himes' books, but neither one was interested in *Invisible Man*. "How about this one?" I asked, holding up several copies of Ellison's book for them to see.

"Near on five hunnert pages," answered Wentworth. "Too long, man. We done already looked at it." I tried to let it go. Books in hand, I turned away and talked to myself: Let them make their own choices . . . it's Friday afternoon and this is candyland . . . be their chauffeur and keep out of their way. But I couldn't refrain, not even for five hundred pages. Of all the books I have read, only Dostoyevsky's *The Idiot* and Ellison's *Invisible Man* have ever caused me to reread every word and every sentence. If I possessed a better memory, each word in Ellison's book would be imprinted on it. Instead, I can only turn to passages that move me most. "Listen," I said, "let me read you something." They stood patiently while I read the following paragraph:

When Ras yelled, "Hang him!" I let fly the spear and it was as though for a moment I had surrendered my life and begun to live again, watching it catch him as he turned his head to shout, ripping through both cheeks, and saw the surprised pause of the crowd as Ras wrestled with the spear that locked his jaws. Some of the men raised their guns, but they were too close to shoot and I hit the first with Tarp's leg chain and the other in the middle with my brief case, then ran through a looted store, hearing the blanging of the burglar alarm as I scrambled over scattered shoes, upturned showcases, chairs —back to where I saw the moonlight from the rear door ahead.

I stopped, and without looking at their faces pushed a copy of the book into each of their boxes. Then I walked past them and pretended to look at books on the shelves. What, after all, could Ralph Ellison teach them about being invisible? I felt self-disgust such as I have seldom known. I had deliberately chosen a violent passage to seduce them into reading the book.

I followed in their wake until I saw Wentworth take one of Murray Leinster's books, *The Aliens*. "You like science fiction, Wentworth?" I asked.

"Like what?"

"Books like that one?"

"Don't know. Ain't never read this'n."

"Why did you choose it?"

"Ain't *aliens* people who don't belong?"

"Yes," I said, seeing the eloquent shrug of his shoulders as he turned away to pursue himself in the colorful covers and sometimes deceptive titles on the shelves. I could provide the Cadillac, books, a visit to the airport . . . but they were the ones who provided the education. Perhaps I too could learn to see a title like *The Aliens* through other eyes.

If *Up the Down Staircase* was about teaching and going to school, then they weren't interested. If I thought it was a good book, well, I could think so if I wanted to. But they knew what it was like without reading it. No argument, no persuasion was possible. Just as no book about aliens could be happy, no book about school could be good. Their expertise was painfully gained and absolutely unchallengable. Belle Kaufman's book stayed on the shelf.

Not until Cleo asked me to hold her box for a moment did I see her pile of "Black" books and realize what she had done. Together with *The Souls of Black Folk*, *Black Like Me*, *Black Men in the White House*, and *Black Boy*, were *Black Beauty*, *Black Arrow*, *Black Treasure*, *Black Tiger*, and

Black Amber. I knew the first four because I had read them as an adult, and the next two because I had read them as a child. A quick glance at the last three and I was ready to explain to her that arrows, treasures, tigers, and amber can be black without being beautiful. Though I was ready to explain, I didn't. A hard-learned lesson is that it is possible to explain too much; where the possibility exists, teachers usually take advantage of it. If I didn't want to share Belle Kaufman's fate, I had to learn forebearance.

We collected Rubbergut, Snapper, and Uncle Wiggly, and made our way back to Mr. Ottenstein's office. The children were silent, exhausted. They had spent themselves in the acquisition of books and they carried their boxes gripped tightly in tired hands. When we reached his office, he was elsewhere in the building; a carton of milk for each child and one for me surrounded a large plate of cookies on the table that had held the mutilated book. The children needed no prompting; accepted, they were accepting. If not expanding, at least their world is expansive. Because it is so sparsely furnished, it has room for much that is new and unexpected. It even has room for undemanding generosity.

"What are them for?" Snapper moved his head toward plaques on the wall.

"Mr. Ottenstein got them for being a philanthropist."

"Yeah?" His response was slow and wary. Only an hour before, in this same room, we had been talking about edible books.

"A philanthropist is a man who uses his money to help other people who can't help themselves." Teachers have the teaching disease. I could have said that he got the awards because he helped people. But I had to teach the meaning of that word. No wonder children avoid conversations with teachers whenever they can.

"He jus' *give* it to 'em?"

"Yes. Through some organization."

"Like the welfare?"

"No. That's government money. He gives his through private groups. Like the one that gave him that award."

Snapper got up to read the plaque hanging behind Mr. Ottenstein's desk. As he read aloud the citation from the United Jewish Appeal, I realized that our visit had come full circle.

7

THE FIRST TIME a member of the gang volun-
tarily spoke to me in school was when Cleo came to me in
the hall with a folded piece of paper. "You know them people?" she asked.

I opened the paper and saw the names John Couch Adams
and Urbain Leverrier written on it. I had never seen them
before.

"Strangers to me," I said.

"Reckon they are," she said. "They the ones find Neptune."

"Maybe," I said, feeling defensive. "But didn't Einstein
predict Neptune would be found before anybody found it?"

"He didn't have nothin' to do with it. Them the people
what did the perdictin'."

I had never seen her face so animated or her eyes so bright.
But they weren't lighted by any expression that might have
been in mine had our positions been reversed. What would I
have felt if I had been able to catch authority so far out?
Victory? Glee? Her face, surprisingly gentle, reflected neither. I started to hand back the piece of paper.

"It yours," she said, pushing it back at me. "Don't cost you
nothin'."

Watching her walk away down the hall, I realized that she had checked my story and my facts in order to help me. The names on the paper were a gift of repayment for the Cadillac, the cop in the airport, the visit to District News . . . no, *repayment* was my term, not hers. She was simply taking care of me, this wise child in a school with faculty, curriculum, and visiting expert unfit to meet her needs. At that moment, I think, the idea of asking her help first occurred to me.

The month was January and I had decided to continue my battle with the faculty as it was, impossible as it was, during the second semester. My decision was pure stubborness, for I had no good reason to hope that new converts were at hand. Aware that I was acting irrationally because I was angry, that the sensible course would be to admit defeat and request transfer of a dozen teachers, I made a desperate connection between Cleo's act of charity and words my friend had used to close our first conversation about her gang: "You get them on your side. They be a real help to you around here." Obtaining their help began to seem like my only hope for making change in the school.

The weekly meetings had come to be a physical symbol of my battle. On an irregularly alternating schedule I met each Thursday either with the entire faculty, excluding most (a few chose to attend) of the teachers of nonacademic subjects, or with a group composed solely of all English and social studies teachers. With some notable exceptions, the smaller group had chosen to participate in the experiment, which in its first stage required substitution of newspapers, magazines, and paperbound books for customary texts. No one knew better than I what willpower total abstinence from those texts required. Having once before suffered with a faculty through fearful pangs of withdrawal, I had no illusions about the ease of the commitment I was seeking. Even without illusions, however, I was unprepared for the depth of hostility displayed by some teachers.

My meetings with the full academic faculty were held in a very large classroom with chairs rearranged to suit the group. Invariably most English and social studies teachers sat toward the front of the room; invariably the group graded itself toward the back of the room on the basis of individual feelings about practices I was proposing. The rear quarter of the room, containing perhaps a fifth of the faculty, looked to me by the end of an hour's meeting like a single glowering eye.

Ten or a dozen teachers in a faculty of fifty-odd is a large number to despair of, but I had given them up for lost. I may have lost them on the day I responded to a leading question by answering that the worst enemy of lower-class schoolchildren, especially black children, is middle-class schoolteachers, especially black teachers. An audible gasp came from several teachers seated in the back of the room. I should have treasured that gasp because it was the last response I was able to elicit from them.

Cleo dissuaded me of my belief about Einstein on Thursday morning. That afternoon I had my worst meeting with the faculty. The day had gone steadily downhill from the highpoint of Cleo's research; it struck bottom when a reasonably good-natured but remarkably dull teacher made her first contribution in many weeks to the discussion. One of the convinced English teachers was praising cooperative teaching, especially cooperation in teaching literacy, when her colleague (not an English teacher) interrupted to declare slowly, emphatically, painfully: "I *know* I'm never going to be any good at teaching reading." I think I may actually have groaned aloud as I heard the ghost exorcised in September rattle its chains in January.

Far worse than that single, benighted comment was the

outpouring it released. For the first time I saw the extent of ill will my program was causing between individuals and factions within the faculty. No one is less forgiving of the unenlightened than recent converts; equally, no one is more immovable than tenured teachers who believe their competence to be in question. The clash between moved and immovable reached epic proportions that January afternoon. Through it all wove the plaintive chorus of the teacher who would never be any good at teaching reading. No one was able to convince her that she would never be asked to teach reading. In fact, no one was able to convince anyone of anything.

No one, that is, except the woman who arranged to walk downstairs with me after the meeting. She, too, was on her way to the principal's office, she said, and she would walk with me because there was something she thought it only right that I should know. I have long since learned to be wary of what follows such introductions, especially from people who have no reason to wish me well. This woman sat somewhere in the middle of the Thursday afternoon meeting (after five months I had everyone classified according to room position) and limited her contributions to various elevations of her eyebrows, which now rose inexorably toward her hairline as she delivered her warning.

Perhaps I should have anticipated her subject, but I didn't. I have since told this story to friends teaching in public schools and a number of them have known immediately what she perceived as her duty. A former student of mine, now an experienced teacher, looked at me with some amazement and asked gently, "But you weren't *surprised*, were you?" But I was surprised. More than that, I was completely unprepared; my shock and outrage must have shown in my face, perhaps even in my words, though I cannot remember what I said, because the woman came close to scurrying as she disappeared down the hall.

Her warning was about consorting with Cleo and her gang. It was the talk of the school, she reported, that I often took children riding in my car on Thursday or Friday afternoons and someone really should tell me what I was getting myself into. She had debated with herself whether or not to say anything, but she just couldn't *stand* to see me *innocently* involved with that kind of child. Quite apart from the question of whether it was advisable to know children out of school at all, which she and many others happened to think was a *very* bad idea, there was the fact that Cleo was probably no better than she should be—did I understand?—and gossip in the faculty was capable of saying almost *anything*. She would have nothing to do with such talk, of course, but there *were* people who. . . .

As I understood what she was talking about, I could feel my face get hot and my neck begin to swell. I must have looked as homicidal as I felt because she broke off in the middle of a sentence and moved away from me down the hall with increasing speed. I found I had to sit for a few minutes in the principal's outer office before I felt able to keep my appointment with him.

8

AFTER OUR TRIPS to National Airport and District News, we made another journey on a Thursday afternoon to the National Gallery of Art. This time, however, I had a double handicap: My car was a Ford instead of a Cadillac, and I was uncertain of the Gallery's potential entertainment value for the children. The Ford was a product of necessity, but the Gallery was a result of choice. Washington is a sightseer's paradise; having lived within fifty miles for twenty years, I am familiar with what it offers. I am also aware that the National Gallery has given me more pleasure than the rest of Washington combined. I made the decision to take Cleo and her gang there in the same way I chose my clothes for the Garnet-Patterson School.

When we opened the Maxey penal school in Michigan, I had little choice of how I would dress for daily meetings with faculty and frequent encounters with boys. Because I had a full teaching schedule at the University, I was obliged to dress alike for training school and university. Either I came to my own lectures, meetings, and conferences directly from Maxey, or I reversed the procedure. Had I been free to choose, I would have dressed down for the penal school. Had

I been free to choose, I would have made the wrong choice.

I would have dressed down because of inexplicable ideas about equality, acceptability, good form—all the condescending cruelty that breeds distrust and hatred between human beings. I would have dressed down simply because I was afraid to dress up, and I would have lost one of my most effective levers with the boys at Maxey. I soon discovered that they felt about fine threads as I once felt about big cars: it's nice to know that someone has them. If someone now, then you later.

The most successful part of my disguise as an expert at Maxey had been my clothes; the disguise was no less efficient on Tenth Street. In both places they brought me double advantage by serving at least two purposes: They were always good for a few words of conversation, and they *represented me to the children as I am.* Nothing, I think, can be more important to a teacher (or a parent) than the freedom which that second advantage allows.

The language adults use with children is an example— usually a negative one—of the advantage I have in mind. I have been asked by many teachers and parents about the advisability of adopting part of their children's current language. My answer is that *conscious* adoption is a probable error for at least two reasons. First, a child's language in an adult's mouth can embarrass a child and cause him to be suspicious of an adult's motives. To what purpose such a mask? A child is bound to ask the question and is unlikely to arrive at a charitable answer. Second, hip terms in a square mouth often function as an irritant in the ear of those to whom they rightfully belong. Such language usually evolves in part as a protective device, a cover designed to hide the private life of the user from the prying eye of the beholder. Unauthorized usage of the cover can make an unwelcome intruder of the user.

I would like to emphasize the qualification of *conscious*

adoption. The teacher or parent who finds a few words used by his students or children making their way into his language should neither be guarded nor insecure about his vocabulary. Children are as quick to appreciate the genuine flattery of occasional imitation as they are to resent the questionable motives of planned intrusion. A teacher who admires a student's new garment and says "sweet threads" can be altogether right or equally wrong. The discrimination lies in the effort, not the words. Because this criterion applies to all interaction with children—within a broad range, what you do matters no more than the ease with which you do it— I decided to take the five of them to the National Gallery. It was the most natural place for me to go on a free Thursday afternoon in Washington.

What I would like to report is that monumental buildings and great paintings rank with airplanes and paperbound books in the hierarchy of objects pleasing to children. With other children, they may, though I doubt it; my five companions found them tolerable, even mildly interesting or momentarily absorbing, but there was no contest between National Airport/District News and National Gallery. The picture of Rubbergut sitting in that magnificent rotunda hunched over *Tarzan and the Ant Man* is graven forever in my memory. Writ large beside it is Snapper's request, when we came out of the Gallery, to drive across nearby Fourteenth Street bridge so that we could see some airplanes. What he needed, he said, was to "get a little action 'fore the sun go down."

The best experience anyone had during our visit to the National Gallery fell to Wentworth and had nothing to do with the Gallery's treasures. We had walked down the broad main steps of the building and across the green parkway of the Mall to our car. I had parked on the street in a large space between two automobiles; as we left the car, Wentworth patted its hood and declared softly that he sure would like to try parking it sometime. Surprised, I asked him if he knew how to drive. Equally surprised, he had answered, "Sure. Don't ever'body?"

I remembered his words as we left the Gallery and approached the car. When I saw who was standing on the nearby grass, I had the beginnings of an idea. "Wentworth," I said, "do you really think you could park that Ford I'm driving?"

"Piece a candy."

"Anybody ever let you park their car?"

"Sure. Four-fi' times."

"Back-up parking?"

"Naw. Just slid 'em up to the curb. But I can do 'er. You jus lemme try."

"Can't do that. If you don't have a driver's license or a learner's permit, I can't let you get behind the wheel. But maybe I know someone who can." The man on the grass was a man on a horse—a mounted policeman whom I had often greeted and spoken with when I came to visit the Gallery. All cops don't roust black kids in airports. This one was a pleasant, well-spoken man, observant enough to note my frequent Thursday and Friday visits in rented cars and interested enough, after our first conversations, to ask what brought me from Michigan to Washington with such regularity. When I told him why and where I was doing my work, he told me what he knew about the lives of impoverished kids in the city of Washington. He was trying to be helpful, and he was. I was grateful, and I stopped to talk with him whenever I could.

This time I left the kids standing by the car while I went to speak to him about Wentworth and his desire to park our rented Ford. My interest in improving the quality or frequency of Wentworth's illegal driving was minimal, but I was

interested in changing what I could of the children's feelings
about police. As with Cleo's anti-Semitism, talk seemed to
me far less useful than example. And I was unhappy about
the negative role a policeman had played in gaining me confidence and affection from the gang. In the long run, the
price was too high. There is a difference between resisting
unnecessary interference and diminishing necessary authority; recognizing the difference, important for preservation of
order in any world, is critical to survival in the world
inhabited by Cleo and her gang.

He didn't agree quickly to what I wanted him to do. Perhaps he wouldn't have agreed at all had I not told him the
story of the airport. When he decided to try to right the
balance—if that's what he decided; at least he agreed to
watch an unlicensed driver attempt to park a car—he turned
his horse and rode slowly down the green parkway toward
the children lounged against the car. The effect upon them of
the approaching horse and rider was galvanic.

Uncle Wiggly was scared quiet. Weeks later, inadvertently,
in a conversation about something else, I discovered that he
had never been close to a horse before, much less had the
opportunity to pat its chest and have it sniff his hand. Of the
five, he was most reluctant to approach horse and rider. At
the time I attributed his hesitation to the rider's identity; I
knew too little to understand that the *size* of the horse had
frightened him almost to the point of fleeing. It had taken
strong nerves and a stronger fear of disgrace for him to
stand his ground.

If Uncle Wiggly was scared, Wentworth was incredulous.
Though his dearest wish at the moment was to drive that car,
he could not bring himself to believe that a cop would watch
him drive a car he did not own with a license he did not
possess and not bust him for something. Once more I had
miscalculated the effect of a familiar symbol upon the

unfamiliar life of a child. For a strange, desperate few minutes I thought I would be unable to overcome the strength of Wentworth's feelings, even with help from a new, bright red Ford.

The Ford won, but barely. For a moment I was outside of myself and the group, watching what appeared to be a tableau in ice slowly freezing and thawing: Each child, in his own way, was greatly affected by the unaccustomed nearness of horse and policeman. Each forced himself to make overtures to the horse and each acknowledged his name as I introduced him to its rider. But the mechanical overtures and acknowledgments were utterly discontinuous, having no apparent connection with the child's ongoing life or with his voluntary responses. Given their free choice, I think the three younger ones would simply have run for it. Cleo and Wentworth may have managed a more dignified pace of retreat, but retreat it would have been for all of them had they not forced themselves to remain in the neutral ground between horse and car.

Even when Wentworth got behind the wheel and started the motor, the kids were of two minds. Suffering from split vision, one eye on the mounted policeman and the other on the car, one part of them saying *run!* while the other froze their feet in place, they were pitiful and unusually pliable in their indecision. I herded them out of harm's way as Wentworth pulled away from the curb to position the car for his first attempt at back-up parking.

When next I returned to the Gallery and sought out the "horsecop" (Snapper's name for him, picked up and used for the rest of the year by all the gang), I was interested to discover how different the incident had appeared to each of us. His talk was of Cleo while my memory was of Wentworth. He remembered the only real action of our encounter, for it was Cleo who had enough presence of mind to step off the curb into the back of the parking space when a small car unexpectedly began to nose its way into the same area which Wentworth was about to occupy with the Ford. The driver of the small car meant no harm; she obviously had not understood that Wentworth was preparing to back into the space, for she had just seen him leave it. When she saw Cleo suddenly walk in front of her car, she stepped hard on the brake and thereby undoubtedly avoided a collision; for Wentworth, oblivious, was entirely absorbed in clearing the rear end of the car at the front of the parking space. It is a tribute to his concentration and testimony to his speed that the woman removed her car from the space and Cleo stepped back on the curb without Wentworth ever knowing that they had been a few feet behind him.

He parked beautifully, not once but five times. Had he pulled out for a sixth try, we would all have thrown our chilled bodies into the empty space to keep him out. But it wasn't necessary; having had all the joy he could stand for one afternoon, he turned off the motor and just sat for a moment looking at nothing. Then, as the others hurried to enter the car and avoid the evening chill, he got out and slowly came around the car to stand in front of the policeman's right stirrup. No one said anything as he rubbed his hand several times over the horse's neck. Finally he patted the horse and said, looking at the man's booted leg, "I been wantin' to do that a *long* time." It was all he could bring himself to say, but it was enough. He was as quiet as Rubbergut, who was asleep, all the way back to Tenth Street.

9

EACH MORNING, before school opened, we received 450 copies of *The Washington Post* in its "bulldog" edition at Garnet-Patterson. That many free newspapers for a single school would be a remarkable gift from any publisher; from the *Post*, it was extraordinary. When I first approached Raoul Blumberg, then assistant to the publisher, he told me that the *Post*'s tradition was to give no free copies at all. Even the publisher paid for his subscription. With so unvarying a policy, the newspaper was able to avoid dilemmas of choice amongst equally worthy applications.

Had Mr. Blumberg not believed it was time for the *Post* to change its policy, my request would have gotten nowhere. Had a number of his colleagues not believed the same, he and I would have been lonely advocates. As it was, "English In Every Classroom" was built in Garnet-Patterson on a mountain of daily newsprint. Without the *Post*, it would have been built on nothing at all; both the federal and local segments of our budget remained unfunded through the entire first semester, and I was reluctant to accept fully Mr. Ottenstein's offer of books and magazines before being certain of future funding.

The newspapers were an enormous success with the children, but they were something less with the teachers. The children liked everything about them including the relatively large number of typographical errors in the edition we were using. When I asked for this particular edition, *Post* executives had been unhappy. It was, after all, their earliest and worst. As first edition on the streets of a morning paper, the "bulldog" is rapidly composed and even more rapidly proofed. Consequently, its errors are many and often spectacular. Nothing more certainly guarantees its popularity with young readers.

What could be more exhilarating for a child than to find adult grammar or spelling in error? For the adolescent to discover patterns and reflections of his own imperfections in the successful adult world (very different from finding them in the failed adults whom he knows too well) is to build his faith in the possibility that such a world may also have room for him. The children gloried in finding misspellings; Cleo and Wentworth were a microcosm of the school in their daily contest to find the most misspelled words. Of course Cleo had the great advantage of being able to read the newspaper openly in her classrooms where it was being used as a textbook. Wentworth was finding it more and more difficult to keep his literacy under cover.

But if children were of one mind about the newspaper, teachers were far from unanimous. Their principal had led the drive to impound old textbooks behind the bookroom's locked door. As he well realized, that door deprived teachers of more than textbooks. In addition to accumulated years of lesson plans, the books represented a school credo held by many teachers and rejected by most children: They were sign and symbol of the belief that *improvement* is self-justifying and requires no motivation other than itself.

Perhaps nowhere is this belief and its destructive effects more clearly to be seen than in the customary choice of reading materials for classrooms in all subjects. To take the best example with the worst results: Tens of thousands of English teachers in high schools all over the United States teach at least one of Shakespeare's plays to each of their classes. Usually they are sensible enough to choose a play with a strong story line—*Julius Caesar, Macbeth, Othello, The Merchant of Venice*—and to open their defense of using Shakespeare by arguing that even if students don't appreciate the poetry, they find the stories exciting. Furthermore, they argue, the plays are *good* to read in the sense that they embody universal moral truths persuasively presented. Finally, and most important, that they are *fine* literature is acknowledged by everyone. Everyone, that is, but children.

The first argument is born of need and convenience— children do want action; the plays have it—but it is insufficient and unconvincing. It is insufficient because the action is hidden beneath language that is often impenetrable for children, and it is unconvincing because it is a deceptive prelude to the dominant argument for using Shakespeare: Universal moral truths embodied persuasively in fine literature are *improving*, and everyone knows that such improvment is the ultimate and real business of the schools.

I have deliberately chosen to base this condemnation of customary school practice on a Victorian theory of public school function. The response I hope to evoke is the apparently reasonable one that asks for a response to American schools in the seventies that is more understanding than this ancient criticism seems to imply. After all, as everyone knows, *improvement* as a standard of action is dead as decorum. Why whip tired horses and rattle ghostly chains to belabor the schools? They have problems enough without facing baseless charges of antiquarianism.

But to the misfortune of both student and society, the charges are not baseless. The faculty at Garnet-Patterson *as a group* was representative of urban school faculties across the nation. No demographic peculiarity had mis-shapen it nor administrative whim crippled it. Individual teachers were indistinguishable from their counterparts in fifty or a hundred large cities in the United States. And they were undeniably antiquarians, collecting, savoring, preserving for their students' edification and pleasure "the best that has been thought and written" in time past. Their final standard of judgment was survival: Since literature that survives the test of time is likely to be good literature, children exposed to such literature are likely to profit from it. Though they live their professional lives surrounded by evidence of the flaw in their equation, most of them act upon the assumption of its validity as though it were gospel.

Two women teachers carried the Word to me one day at lunchtime. Both were English teachers and both were "very happy" with my program but. . . .

"Dr. Fader, I've been telling Dorothy here that you've got a big problem with teachers who won't cooperate, so you have to make your point by saying things you don't really mean."

I admitted I might do that sometimes and asked what she had in mind. I counted her as a mild partisan of the program, while her friend was one of the uncommitted.

"Well, like teaching Shakespeare. Why, you even had *me* worried until I asked our English Supervisor what courses you teach at the university. When she told me you teach Shakespeare, I *knew* I was right."

She proceeded to reassure me that she and Dorothy and the "right kind of teacher" would understand from now on that I was just using Shakespeare as an exaggerated example of what I didn't want teachers to be doing. They would understand that it was the only way for me to make my point "with some of the slower teachers." She actually patted me on the arm, delighted at being part of a superior conspiracy.

The conspiracy which delighted her was created and nurtured entirely within the confines of her own imagination. She was so relieved to discover that I taught Shakespeare at the University of Michigan because she could not believe I meant what I said about teaching Shakespeare to junior high school students reading several years beneath their grade level. In answer to a direct question at a faculty meeting, I cited our experience at the prison school as sufficient reason for preferring the newspaper to Shakespeare for increasing both pleasure and performance in reluctant readers.

Did I mean to say that both should be used, but the newspaper used first?

No, I did not mean to say that. In most junior high school English classrooms, Shakespeare should not be taught at all. It is possible that there are teachers inspired enough to make Shakespeare live for functional illiterates and inept readers; it is also possible that a few students can read Shakespeare with pleasure. But if one omits inspired teachers and accomplished readers, who together can not form more than a miniscule proportion of any junior high school faculty and student body, then Shakespeare is far too difficult to be included within the curriculum.

I had no idea of the impact of my words upon the gathered English teachers until one of the more belligerent ones asked loudly, in the midst of another teacher's comment on a different subject, what kind of school was it that only taught children how to read the newspaper? Had I anticipated the question, I might have been more guarded in my response. Instead, I answered—also loudly—that it was a better school than one which *didn't* teach them how to read the newspaper. The remainder of the meeting was louder than any that had gone before.

After risking so much to state and restate the case for the newspaper and against fine literature, I had before me

probable evidence that no statement of mine would be sufficient to dissuade many teachers from their cherished beliefs
about the real nature of their task. If children were not in
school to be improved, why indeed were they there? Education in literacy was important, but education in quality was
more important. If the question lay between common literacy and uncommon literature, then the answer would have
to be very carefully considered. It was not at all clear that
distinguished literature should be sacrificed to needs of
undistinguished children.

Though I had been patted on the arm, it was clear that
my arm was simply a substitute for my head, which was
out of reach. I have never in my life felt so ineffectual as
when the two women smiled happily at me, one conveyed
her affection with a pat, and both left secure in the belief
that ancient ordering of values in the universe was not
really being challenged by anyone. Mine was only an apparent attack, based upon necessary hyperbole rather than
heretical belief, and all good people could rally to my side,
secure in knowledge that Shakespeare was my brother in
arms.

Many of my encounters with the frozen stance of public
school teachers had been and would yet be more fierce and
less tolerable than that brief exchange in the Garnet-
Patterson halls. But none has ever been more chilling to my
hopes for significant change in school philosophy and practice. What my lady friend, the patter, had given me was an
unobstructed view of the height and breadth built into walls
protecting many a schoolteacher's concept of teaching literacy. For the first time in my five months at the school I felt
that the walls might be too high and strong to be scaled or
breeched by me. I do, however, owe a considerable debt to
those two English teachers, for it was my encounter with
them that finally convinced me to go to Cleo and her gang
for help.

10

CLEO WAS JUST "coming up fourteen" when I met her. I use her words because of the view of life they reflect. Where I might have spoken of "coming up roses," she used the phrase to express a simple fact of age. Or perhaps she recognized that for her the accumulation of fourteen years was no simple fact, that survival under adverse conditions can itself be a satisfaction. If her phrase implied something of delight and wonder, the implication was fully justified. Her survival was remarkable both in its fact and in its condition.

When I met her, Cleo was in the ninth grade and her gang was in its third year. She had organized it when she and Wentworth were in seventh grade at the junior high school. Snapper, Rubbergut, and Uncle Wiggly were still in sixth grade at a nearby elementary school when Cleo recruited them. Age and grade meant less than proximity, for the children lived near each other and their arrangement grew out of the neighborhood, not out of school. More important, it grew out of mutual need.

Except for information reluctantly given me by the man who knew something about Cleo and her gang, and the warning eagerly given me by the woman who knew nothing, I had no knowledge of Cleo's sexual relationship to the boys. None of them ever confided in me and I neither searched for nor obtained confirmation of the intercourse they were said to be sharing. It was, I admit, information I was glad not to have. No less than the teacher of *good* literature, I was driven by a brutal demand called "the *right* thing to do." In this case, I had no idea what it was.

Having been relieved by ignorance of the need for moral action, I was free to try to understand the children as they were rather than as I wanted them to be. Instead of spending my energies on improving them, I was able to devote myself to identifying them. The effort seemed worthwhile, for they and their peers formed the *corpus* whose discomforts of rhetoric and diseases of reading my program hoped in part to remediate. In order to comprehend movements of the body, I began by trying to understand motives of the head:

Who was this girl named Cleo who could organize four eleven- and twelve-year-old boys into a group that remained cohesive for three full years, a group that kept its identity in a fractionated world that disintegrated at a touch? First of all, she was a plain, direct, intelligent girl who was remarkably unafraid in a world full of fearful children and adults. If sex was her organizing principle, she may have depended upon it to retain her dominant position in the gang. She may have, but I doubt it. I doubt it not because I undervalue the power of sex amongst adolescents, but because Cleo was in command of the group when she was dependent upon other attributes. Her considered forebearance and her absolute clarity were but two of those strengths. More important than both was the special sensitivity which caused her to choose her four companions.

The boys she chose shared more than Cleo, more than

age, neighborhood, poverty, and race. They each had an individual loneliness about them, an isolation symbolized by the deliberate deception Wentworth practiced in his English class. As the year wore on, I discovered that each was more like the others than they were like the typical children who inhabited Garnet-Patterson School.

Wentworth was toughest, most resilient, while Snapper was most brittle. What was remarkable was that two such different children should have learned to protect themselves from the damage of collision with the juggernaut called school by adopting similar evasive techniques. Where Wentworth feigned ignorance and passivity, Snapper pretended sullen stupidity. Though I became reconciled to Wentworth's deception, I was never able to accept Snapper's act. Nothing human has repelled me more than the protective dullness that glazed his eyes as he responded with stupid ill-nature to the simplest classroom question or request. Sometimes it seemed impossible that the dull, pettish child in the classroom could be the bright, excited boy I came to know in the streets.

Two incidents in two consecutive school days were painful examples of the discrepancy between the boy as he was and the boy as he revealed himself to the world he despised. The first occurred in the cafeteria during a Thursday lunch hour when a big, heavy boy had an epileptic seizure. His plunge to the floor was so sudden and his convulsions so violent that he might have harmed himself greatly had Snapper not intervened. The boy had been walking back to his table with a full tray from the cafeteria line. I was eating my lunch and talking to the teacher sitting across from me when my attention was caught by a tray suspended in midair and a head disappearing beneath a table top. By the time I crossed twenty feet that separated me from the stricken boy, Snapper had run between jammed chairs and tables, had fished the epileptic's tongue from his mouth, had taken his head on his lap and was calling for something to place between the boy's jaws to prevent him from biting his tongue.

Wentworth told me that afternoon about Snapper's two full brothers and one sister who were "fallin' sick." Wentworth wasn't sure whether Snapper lived with his real father or mother, but whichever one was gone was taken off by the same trouble. Snapper, the only child of the original marriage who was free of the disease, was the eldest of four and responsible for taking care of his brothers and sister whenever their parents weren't home, which was often. He had some practice, Wentworth said, at what he had done in the cafeteria that day.

Friday gave me a full view of the other Snapper. I wrote the three following sentences on the back of an envelope with stamps canceled in November of 1965:

"Isn't the truth just easier to tell? You should try it, William. You'll find it costs less in the long run."

The envelope was all the paper I had with me when I passed a classroom and heard the conversation between a boy and his math teacher that concluded with those sentences. Perhaps the oddest dimension of the conversation is that the boy's name was not William; or, even stranger, that the teacher knew his name was not William, but persisted in calling him William nonetheless.

William's real name was Willie. His friends called him Snapper, a nickname derived from his proficiency with rubber bands and paper clips. A few of his teachers called him Snapper, while all the rest called him Willie. All the rest, that is, except his math teacher. She called him William because, as she told me, it did not matter that the name on his birth certificate was Willie; his name *should* have been William, and if his parents hadn't been so ignorant they would have named him properly: "Willie is not a proper name," she told me. "It's a diminutive, not fit to be used outside family and friends."

"How about the female name of Willie?" I asked her. "Like in Willie Mae?"

"Ignorance again," she answered. "Obviously it should should have been Willa. As in Willa Cather."

Obviously. All ignorance. But perhaps less obvious is the bone-deep ignorance of the teacher's three sentence conclusion to her dialogue with Snapper. The conversation took its apparent beginning from a piece of unsubmitted homework and a question. The missing homework was Snapper's; the question belonged to the teacher: "Why didn't you do your homework last night, William?" she asked as he passed her on his way into the corridor.

"My gramma was took bad las' night and I had to set up with her," he replied, looking at a spot on the door frame a foot to the left of her head.

"Sick all evening?" she asked, deceptively sympathetic.

"Yes, ma'am."

"William, you're a liar."

"No ma'am."

"Standing here right in front of me, lying to my face. I saw your grandmother in church last night and she looked just fine."

"Yes ma'am."

And then the deluge: Come to see me after school. Yes ma'am. You tell such silly lies. Yes ma'am. The truth is easier to tell. It costs less. Yes ma'am. All the time she speaks, his eyes never leave the door frame.

The math teacher is right, of course. Snapper is a liar; what's worse, he tells foolish, transparent lies. But she isn't right about anything else that has to do with the boy and his lying. For what she doesn't understand is that she is responsible for making a liar of him. She and all the men and women who ask him unanswerable questions to which, mercilessly, they require answers. His requirement is survival, which makes him no different from his math teacher and all the rest of us; like her, and like us, he will do what he must in order to survive.

In order to survive, Snapper must lie. He knows he must, and will tell you so if you ask him. But of course it is not our style to ask a Snapper or a Willie about himself; instead, we ask ourselves about Willie and, willy-nilly, we become experts on Willie.

If asked, he will tell you he's a liar. As he told me when I asked him at lunchtime after his math class. "Thing is," he said reflectively, "I would of said I set with my ma iff'n I'd known she seen my gramma." No regrets for the lie; regrets only for not having told the best available lie. Obviously an immoral child. Or what may be more to the point—obviously an immoral teacher.

Does that seem too strong? Immoral child? Well, perhaps. But immoral teacher? The judgment seems irresponsibly made, the word wrongly used. . . . Yes, I think so too, *but when applied to the child, not to the teacher.* The teacher's words are clearly immoral, for they are the sufficient cause of an immoral act in the child—the act of lying. Proof of such an accusation is important; understanding the proof is crucial to the arts of teaching and the acts of a compassionate human being.

Let me begin my proof with some patently absurd questions whose absurdity may depend upon your viewpoint:

Do poor children tell more lies than rich children? Do poor black children tell more lies than poor white children? Does darker skin not only screen the sun out but keep the truth in?

"Why didn't you do your homework last night, William?

Isn't the truth easier to tell? Doesn't it cost less? Why don't you tell the truth?"

Proof of the accusation of immorality lies in examination of these questions. Begin with the teacher's question to William-Willie-Snapper about his homework. Begin there because that's where the immorality begins. It does not, in spite of appearances and our own self-justifying beliefs, begin with the child's transparent lie about his grandmother. It begins, instead, with the question which demands and accepts no answer other than a lie.

"Come now," my straw man says, "an obvious and acceptable alternative is the truth." Please, I say in response, whose truth do you have in mind—the teacher's or the child's? The teacher's truth is that she is not really asking a question at all. She knows perfectly well that the child has no answer to her question. Even if she wanted him to, he would be unable to respond with a recitation of accumulated traumas which have built so great a barrier between himself and performance. Her question has nothing to do with an attempt to link cause and effect, one customary province of a question, but has all to do with discipline. In her view, if she assigns homework that remains undone and she fails to react to its nonperformance, then she has been derelict in her duty to children and to herself. She is entitled to her view. But she is not entitled to force a child to lie, which is exactly what she has done by asking her question.

The typical child asked such a question has absolutely no idea why he didn't do his homework. He didn't do it because he didn't do it, not because he forgot or didn't understand the assignment or because he had to sit up with his grandmother. He didn't forget because he never intended to remember; he didn't find the assignment incomprehensible because he never tried to comprehend it; and even a death in his family could have no effect upon intentions never intended. Worst of all, the teacher who asks the question *knows all of this*. Admitting it, however, would be to admit the absurdity of burdening such a child with such an assignment. Admitting it could be the first step in a self-searching series of questions which might lead the teacher to change her aims, her expectations, and her practices. Easier by far to make a liar of the child.

Having done so, she then joins one of two classes of experts, her rhetoric of discrimination depending entirely upon her class. One class says (or thinks or implies or acts upon the belief) that "*these people* simply don't value the truth as much as we do;" the other says that "*these children* simply don't seem to be able to tell the truth." The sole difference in distinguishing characteristics between the two classes is that the former is white while the latter is black.

Whether seen as a function of race or age, this view of certain children's capacity for truth is a desperate and indefensible search for justification by teachers whose main desire is to exculpate themselves from responsibility for the liars they create. Do poor children tell more lies than rich children? Of course they do, for more lies are required of them. Do poor black children tell more lies than poor white children? Of course they do; not only are more lies required of them because their poverty is generally more hopeless, but more lies are required of them because more people require them to lie.

Poor white children are required to lie because they are poor; poor black children are required to lie because they are poor and because they are black. The latter requirement is not unique. Ask any of the Boston Irish or New York Jews or Detroit Poles who went to school to their betters, themselves Irish or Jewish or Polish, but *Americanized*. Ask them how it was to come to school with your different clothes and your peculiar accent and have yourself, one generation removed, stand in front of the class and tell you by god to turn American and do it fast! Ask the poor black kids how it is to have a black teacher stand in front of the class and radiate sub-vocal signals which sound endlessly in your ears: "Turn white! Turn white! Turn white!" Ask them how it is, and they may tell you that nothing in the world could be worse.

But that is only a digression, for we still recognize the inalienable right of a minority to persecute itself. What we do not recognize, however, is the torment and brutality of questions like "Isn't the truth easier to tell?" and "Doesn't it cost less?" when asked of children for whom the price of truth is nothing less than self-respect.

When the math teacher asked Snapper a question which was only answerable by "I don't know," an answer which she would have accepted as the truth even if she could not accept it as an excuse, she asked him to encompass a full view of his disastrous relationship to school. When a performance-oriented child doesn't perform and doesn't know why, "I don't know" is no more than a temporary admission of aberrance and failure. A child who can't or won't perform, however, may find the cost of "I don't know" to be far beyond his means. Because it is too dear a confession, he purchases a temporary reprieve with a far less expensive lie.

11

ONE OF THE few times I saw Cleo angry—so angry that she almost lost control of herself—was when Snapper provoked a teacher into name-calling. None of us witnessed the event; all we knew of it was Snapper's report, obliquely delivered, that afternoon. We were sitting in my car, parked on Tenth Street in front of school, when a teacher left the building and crossed the street in front of us.

"She ain't worth nothin'," Snapper said flatly.

"Who?"

"Her. Big Butt."

"What she do on you?"

"Lay a name on me."

"Will-*yum*?" Rubbergut said it with emphasis and with a smile. But Snapper didn't respond.

"What she call you?" Cleo's question required an answer. I was surprised at its sharpness; was there something I had missed? Why did she care what the name was? I thought Snapper felt as I did when he answered mildly—

"It don't matter none."

"You tell me what she say, I tell you iff'n it don't matter

none." I had never heard her use that tone before. She was obviously prepared to be angry, but I was unable to understand why. Did a day pass that some vengeful adult didn't call them a name? It hardly seemed worth the pain to live through one of those incidents again. I was already turning the key in the ignition, hoping that noise and motion would distract them, when Snapper responded to his leader's command:

"She call me a jungle nigger."

We sat in the nearest thing to absolute silence that six people, five of them adolescents, can attain. Drops from a brief rain shower ran soundlessly down the windshield while schoolchildren hurried across the street in front of us. Sitting in the outside front seat, Cleo suddenly brought her fist down hard on the dashboard and her lips moved, though she said nothing I could hear. Then, after a brief pause— the car still soundless—she reached across Wentworth and patted my arm. They couldn't go for a ride, she explained, apology and regret in her voice. They were mighty sorry, but maybe we could all go to that place next week. And she knew it was two times that word had been laid on my ears. It wasn't no way to talk in front of a friend. The three from the back seat were already waiting on the sidewalk when Cleo and Wentworth left me alone in the car.

That was twice I had been patted on the arm and twice I had been left to my own frustration. The first time forced me to realize how thick the scar tissue is that protects experienced school teachers from change; the second time showed me how thin the skin is that protects constantly abused children from their own violence. I knew perfectly well I had witnessed a prelude to vengeance. I knew the teacher, and I knew how well she deserved her reputation for a vicious mouth. I knew the children, and I had seen rage and determination in Cleo's face. Only one product was possible from those volatile elements in combination. Knowing, I was powerless to prevent it.

I was a fool to think I had witnessed a prelude to immediate violence. At least Cleo and Wentworth were too smart for that, if not the others. Which is probably to do the others an injustice, for I believe now that Snapper's reluctance to repeat the teacher's epithet grew out of his foreknowledge of Cleo's response. Whatever the reason, he had not been anxious to provoke immediate retaliation and I should have known better than to fear it. The children were as cautious and circumspect in their vengeance as they were in their friendship.

A month passed before they retaliated. Had the event occurred early in the week, I might not have known of it. Since they acted on a Wednesday, however, it was the teachers' prime topic for conversation on Thursday. What they had done was simple and devastating: They had slashed all four tires on the woman's car, and they had added sand to her gas tank, radiator, and oil system. When I heard about it, I felt only relief. I had been afraid they would act against her person instead of her possessions.

Though I was relieved at the nature of the act, and therefore glad to know of it, I found the knowledge itself an intolerable burden in my relationship to the gang. Before the vandalism occurred, I had expected to ignore whatever happened since the children were certain to make me neither witness nor confidant. I was sure they understood my position too well to give me information I didn't need or want. I have always found adolescents highly selective in what they reveal to adults, and remarkably considerate in that selectivity when they regard those adults as friends.

They revealed nothing to me. My problem was not with them, but with myself. When I heard about the damaged car, I realized how deliberately I had refused to mediate between teacher and gang. It was mediation easy to avoid. No one in the school who had any prolonged contact with the woman had escaped her mouth. If I had agreed to the plan of purging the faculty, she would have been one of the first to go. And of course I had been able to tell myself, a month ago, that I had no evidence of the gang's intent. Only when I felt relief at news of damage to her car rather than to her person did I realize how certain I had been of their intent, and how much a party—though passive—I had been to their act. In spite of my bad conscience, I do not think I would have said or done anything about their vandalism had they not thrust the opportunity upon me.

The opportunity arose from another brief clash between Cleo and Wentworth. An increasing number of these confrontations marked the passage of our year together; what was happening, I think, is that the relationship between them was about to reverse itself and both were searching for new ground on which to stand. As I came to understand this, both became more admirable in my eyes for the genuine kindness with which they treated each other. Especially Cleo, who understood that Wentworth needed help in shedding his outgrown skin.

Occasion for the clash was Wentworth's admiration of Dick Gregory and Cleo's supersensitivity about the word *nigger*. When we went to visit Joe Ottenstein and his District News Company, Wentworth acquired copies of *From the Back of the Bus* and *Nigger*. At the time I thought Cleo had them too, but I was mistaken. She was shocked by the title of *Nigger* and had refused to take any of Gregory's books. I discovered this when Wentworth took *Nigger* out of his pocket one day and passed it to Uncle Wiggly.

"I brung it for you," he said. "Give it back when you done."

"My ma kin read it?" Uncle Wiggly's mother read everything he brought home. He had told us about her when he

met us one Friday after school with three women's magazines rolled up in his hand.

"Sure," Wentworth said, and added expansively, "you
gramma, too, iff'n she wants."

"Ain't fit for nobody," Cleo pronounced emphatically. She
made a pushing motion with her hand, as though shoving
the book away from her.

"How you know?" asked Wentworth. "You ain't never
read it."

"Ain't never gonna read it neither!"

"Then how you know so much?"

"I know."

"Just 'cause he call it *Nigger*, you ain't even gonna find
out what he say?"

"Man use that word, he don't say nothin' I wanna hear."

"Ain't it a good book?" Wentworth was appealing to me.
I was in, whether I wanted to be or not.

"You remember what he writes to his mother?" I asked
Wentworth. He didn't, so I repeated as accurately as I could
the dedication which I now quote from the book: "Dear
Momma—Wherever you are, if ever you hear the word
nigger again, remember they are advertising my book."

"Yeah," Wentworth said. "That's good."

"I like it, too," I said. "He puts that word right where it
belongs."

"It don't belong on no book." Cleo shook her finger at the
book in Uncle Wiggly's hand.

"You're right," I said. "It doesn't belong on a book and it
doesn't belong in anybody's mouth or mind. But it's there.
And it won't disappear because you want it to. It won't
disappear unless you do something about it. Like Dick
Gregory's doing by bringing it out in the open and laughing
at it. That's one way of getting rid of it."

I knew I was walking on thin cover but I was tired of
unnameable and unmentionable things: "You can laugh at

it and it'll disappear. Or you can talk it away. But you can't turn your back on it. It's got to be dealt with. And when you mess up somebody's car after she calls you a jungle nigger, you aren't dealing with it because you aren't teaching her anything. Messing up her car isn't going to cost her any-thing but money."

"Cost her plenty a that."

"You handle it right, you could cost her her job. Insurance takes care of her car. Nothing takes care of her job. When it's gone, it's gone."

"Now how *we* gonna get *her* job?" Cleo, with interest and disbelief.

"You're not. You got sore and lost your chance. You're not the only ones who know how bad she is. But you and the rest of her students are the only ones who can prove it. When she called Snapper a jungle nigger you could all have gone to see the principal. He's a good man and you know it. He'd do something about it."

"You could tell him."

"No, I can't. I can't because I'm white and she's black and I'm a stranger here. She or somebody would swear race was the problem and the whole thing would get lost in black and white. No, not me. It had to be you." I hadn't meant my words to be so final, but they were. A depressed silence wrapped us like a winding sheet. I thought I'd buried the subject, which I hadn't wanted to do, until Snapper revived it with a sad, quiet observation:

"We could have got her *good.*"

"We done it. That car ain't goin' nowhere." Uncle Wiggly, hopefully.

"Naw," Cleo, speaking slowly. "We didn't do *nothin'.* She still here, mean as ever. Messin' on her car didn't keep her from comin'. She still here, niggerin' everybody to death." Then a longer silence before she turned to me and said, "You tell us. You tell us what we kin do."

12

I COULDN'T TELL THEM, then. All I could do
was attempt to reinforce their lively belief in the principal's
fairness and to revive their moribund belief in the system he
represented. No matter where we were or what we were
doing, our conversation would turn to their new concern for
meaningful revenge. Because it is not pleasant to contemplate vengeful children, I almost wrote "meaningful action."
That may be more pleasant, but it is certainly less accurate.
They were no more activists than people of the Old Testament who demanded eye for eye and tooth for tooth. And
they were also like ancient Hebrews who looked upon their
handiwork to find it wanting: For the first time it was clear
to Cleo and her boys that a messed up car was insufficient
and inappropriate repayment for pain they had suffered from
its owner.

Before I had sense enough to ask for their help in my work
at the school, they had already reached their own conclusions
about rewards of real action. Though it is true that I initiated
many early conversations about differences between attack-
ing a car and defeating an enemy, I became an interested by-

stander at later debates. I am aware of the apparent anomaly in attributing debates to children; like so much else in our view of children, the anomaly lies in us rather than in them. I have witnessed not one but several genuine debates amongst Cleo and her boys where both form and product were admirable.

Perhaps the best conversation occurred on a fine and unseasonably warm January day not long before I came to agreement with the gang about their needs and mine within the school. We were sitting on the school steps after everyone had gone home. The children had waited for me after my meeting, which had not been with the full faculty but only with English and social studies teachers, because we had talked about visiting the University of Maryland campus on the first fine day. But even that meeting with only a quarter of the faculty had been overlong and had left us too little January daylight to enjoy the campus. After deciding to go tomorrow if the day were nice, we sat in the sun and talked as we enjoyed the warmth.

Because our conversation was casual, our topic was very familiar. If we did not begin with places I had lived, when we had nothing more important to talk about, then we soon got to the subject and remained there. Nothing else seemed to have so much attraction for the children. I soon discovered that they were far less interested in what I had done than where I had been when I had done it. The discovery may have been hard on my ego but it was easy on our relationship, for it freed me of identity and allowed me to become a conveyor of picture and place.

Their favorite place was San Francisco, their favorite picture the view of that pastel city from Twin Peaks. Each time they asked about it I tried to describe another aspect of the city or its peninsula. Casting about in my memory for something different on this comfortable afternoon, I remembered

Chinese New Year celebrations held in San Francisco's Chinatown and told them about the great dragon that danced through the streets. The picture brought them pleasure and desire. They decided that if the Chinese New Year were celebrated in February, as I thought perhaps it was, then next month they would just leave their nothing school and their nowhere neighborhood (no mention of their city; they never thought of it as theirs) to go out to San Francisco and never come back.

Remembering who they were and where they were momentarily dimmed the brightness of the day. "Ever' year the Year of the Dog 'round here," said Cleo flatly when I told her about the Chinese practice of naming each new year.

"Shit," Snapper said, to no one in particular, "you don't bark loud, you don't never get heard."

The Year of the Dog. The boys liked the image. Rubbergut picked it up and stretched it slowly in the afternoon sun. "Wouldn't be so bad to be a big old tick hound with nothin' to do but eat and sleep and run."

"What you hunt wouldn't scare you weak?" asked Snapper disdainfully. Rubbergut was a notorious coward. The rest of the boys tolerated him because he was Cleo's choice and Snapper's half brother, but his cowardice was like a rat at which they threw stones whenever it showed its head. Rubbergut retreated as Cleo turned the subject to business.

"Ever' year the Year of the Dog here," she repeated. "This school don't teach us nothin' 'cept to bark."

Spontaneously, almost in unison, the boys began to bark. I looked around, suddenly self-conscious, aware that I was a grown man sitting on steps of an unused school entrance with four barking boys and one grinning girl. A man came to the second floor window of a house across the street. I saw a dog farther down the block stop in confusion. I couldn't blame him. We must have been something to see and hear.

"I'd hunt me a teacher," Rubbergut said unexpectedly when the barking had quieted. "I'd hunt me a teacher rabbit and have me a stew."

"What else you put in?" asked Cleo, not unkindly. "Sure be a mighty thin stew iff'n you only got you a teacher rabbit."

"Taste like shit," said Snapper. He had used his favorite word, unself-consciously, for the second time, which was remarkable since he had only recently decided it might be acceptable in my presence. I wished then, as I do now when reconstructing these conversations from notes and memory, that I had been able to use a tape recorder. One myth those tapes would have laid to rest is the fantasy common amongst middle-class teachers that rhetorical discrimination is a proportionate function of advantage. Which is another way of saying that poor kids don't recognize or react as quickly as other kids to the need for different kinds of language in different situations.

The best example I know comes from a penal school, but the lesson begins at Detroit's Northwestern High. A teacher at Northwestern was talking with me outside her classroom about returning to Michigan for a graduate degree. Our conversation was distracted and interrupted by raised voices from the next classroom which grew louder and angrier. Finally we stopped to listen:

"Don't you tell me you didn't throw that eraser. I saw you with my own eyes!"

"Wasn't me. It was *him*! I'm gonna get me a piece of him after school."

"Don't you tell me it was somebody else! It was you. *I* saw you!"

"Shi-i. . . ."

"That's all I'm going to take from you! You and your filthy mouth! Get out of here; I won't let you speak that way to me!"

That's the end of the conversation as I noted it; it had,

however, several more lines, even if at that moment unspoken:

"But I didn't say nothin'...."

"Didn't say *'nothin'*! You know what you said. The whole class heard you. Now get out and don't come back until you can talk like a gentleman."

And so he got out, but he was unlikely to return if it meant meeting her terms and definitions. For her accusation was not that he had used the wrong word, but that he had used it in the wrong place. I did not know her well, but she seemed a reasonable woman in other circumstances. She did not seem the kind to deny that the boy had the word *shit* in his functioning vocabulary, nor would she deny that the word was sometimes appropriate to the context in which he used it. But she would certainly deny that such a word had any place in her classroom. Strangely enough, so would the boy.

One useful way of approaching this apparent contradiction is to ask if that boy (or any boy neither brain-damaged nor desperate) swears as much in school as he does on the street. The answer of course is that he doesn't; he knows he can't talk like that and survive in the classroom. If we concede him this knowledge, then how do we account for his aberrant action? The usual answer is that he succumbs to momentary pressure and "forgets himself." I propose that the usual answer is usually mistaken; furthermore, I believe that if the boy were given a fair hearing, instead of one predisposed to find him wrong, we would discover the fault to be more the teacher's than the child's.

"The teacher's fault? That's ludicrous," says her partisan. "How can it be the teacher's fault? *She* didn't say *shit*."

No, that's true, she didn't. But neither did the boy.

"Of course he did! I heard him and so did you."

You may have; the teacher certainly did; however, I did not. What I did hear him say was "shi-i...." and therein lies a world of difference.

The difference may be more apparent in intent than performance, but it exists and must be accounted for by every ear that believes itself outraged. I learned the difference from Leon Holman, then a teacher in Green Oaks, a maximum security unit in Michigan's juvenile penal system. Leon, now principal of the W. J. Maxey Boys Training School, taught me my first lesson in a subject obscure to me then and obscure to most teachers now—the verbal *intent* of partly vocal children.

Our situation was this: Leon was teaching an English class of eight teen-age boys who had been confined in Green Oaks because they were too difficult to handle in other Michigan penal institutions. On the third day that I watched this gifted teacher at work, he had one student teacher from Eastern Michigan University named Don Williams and two serious problems from Detroit named Superduck and Roy.

Superduck was a big, simple seventeen-year-old boy whose vocal responses were usually limited to a variety of quacks. A typical conversation with Superduck elicited negative, positive, and interrogatory quacks, punctuated with occasional rooster calls, other barnyard noises, and even more occasional human noises resembling words. Under any circumstances, a conversation with Superduck was memorable; in the classroom, with seven unstable boys as witnesses and participants, it approached the indescribable.

On this particular morning, Leon came as close as he dared to lifting Superduck's veil of quacks. While Don worked with the others, Leon concentrated on Superduck. His aim was to engage the boy in a conversation about assigned readings in the form of mimeographed stories written by Leon out of his own experience of the ghetto. He knew Superduck had read at least one of the stories because he had seen him do it. Now the problem was to get him to talk about it in words.

Soon I found I was not the only listener to their conversation. A troubled boy named Roy, unable to concentrate on the lesson Don was teaching, began to participate in Leon's questions and Superduck's answers. Roy's meanness was in direct proportion to the vulnerability of his target; since Superduck's quacks and infrequent roars hid a gentle heart, Roy's abuse increased with his participation. It reached a peak when Superduck allowed as how he knew a Detroit street corner like the one Leon had described in his story.

"Sure he do," commented Roy. "His momma sell her ass on it."

Leon is a big man, but he's quick. He was between Superduck and Roy before Superduck could get out of his seat to avenge a mortal insult. Roy was already on his feet; when Leon shoved him back into his chair, Roy responded with, "Get you hands offa me, you mothah!"

"I get *my* hands on him, I bust him into pieces." It may have been the longest quackless speech Superduck ever made.

"You," Leon said to Roy, one hand on Superduck's shoulder, "You keep your mouth off him. You hear?"

"Shi-i . . .," said Roy, voice full of disdain but body remaining seated. Apparently satisfied, Leon went back to his desk. As far as he was concerned, the incident was finished.

If it was finished for him and the boys, it was still unfinished for me. Leon later completed it, teaching me a brief and unforgettable lesson in the rhetorical discrimination of children:

"What did you think of the boys today?" he asked at lunch.

"The boys? You mean Roy and Superduck?"

"Well, all the boys, but them especially."

"I think you should have let Superduck bust Roy in the mouth. If a kid ever had it coming. . . ."

"Yeah. That Roy is about the meanest kid I've ever seen."

"And the way you let him talk. You're a mighty patient man; I'd have thrown him out of class."

"For what he said to Superduck? Maybe I should have."

"I'm not talking about what he said to Superduck. I'm talking about what he said to *you!*"

"To me?" Genuine surprise. "What did he say to me?"

"You know what he said as well as I do. He called you a motherhumper and his last word after you warned him was *shit.*"

"You think I'd let him get away with that? The class would go high as a kite if I let him talk like that."

I began to feel like we were talking at each other through thick glass. He had been there, just as I had. Why hadn't he heard what I had heard? Maybe enough time in Green Oaks put you permanently out of touch with reality. "Look. I *heard* him. Are you trying to tell me he didn't say *shit* and call you a motherhumper?"

"That's what I'm telling you. He called me a *mothah* and he said *shi-i.* . . . There's all the difference."

"All the difference? What kind of difference? You knew what he meant and so did everybody else in the room."

"Everybody but you. You want to prove it, you ask Don if Roy badmouthed me today." Don had joined us at the table in time to hear Leon's last statement.

"Who was badmouthed?" he asked.

"Leon," I answered. "Today. In class."

"Which class?"

"What is this? A conspiracy to make me think I'm losing my mind? I heard Roy say *shit* to Leon's directions and call him a motherhumper. I tell you I *heard* it."

And so they explained to me that my hearing was bad, not the boy's mouth. If he had wanted to call Leon a *motherhumper,* he wouldn't have called him a *mothah.* If he had meant to say *shit,* he wouldn't have said *shi-i.* . . . Maybe I didn't know that, but everybody else in the classroom did. What Roy was doing was putting a limit on how far he wanted things to go. He was telling anybody who listened that he wasn't asking for expulsion from the classroom. Mean as he was, he would have been surprised and indignant had Leon done more than he did. For Roy had been very careful in his choice of rhetoric to fit the occasion.

That was seven years ago. During those years I have tried to respond to what children say rather than to what I expect or want them to say. Responding to children in this way is not a natural act; I have often been chagrined or embarrassed to discover myself listening to myself (rather than to the child) and answering a question both unasked and unintended. Or, worst of all, I have given an answer that was not only unwanted but unmanageable by the child. In this, as in so much else, adult responses are inferior to children's, for children are usually too wise to burden adults with information they cannot handle.

13

IT WAS SNAPPER'S comment on the taste of teacher stew that took me back to Roy and his classroom language. But Snapper sat in no classroom on that January afternoon in 1966. He sat amongst his companions on the front steps of the school and I was not his teacher but his friend. Or at least I was an acquaintance to be trusted within reasonable limits.

The limits expanded that afternoon as daylight waned. For the first time the children asked me about myself, about where and how I had grown up, about my childhood family in Baltimore and my present family in Ann Arbor. The questions grew out of sudden embarrassment and tenderness of feeling when the conversation turned to teachers, and the children realized that one example of that thin and stringy stew meat was sitting beside them on the school steps.

"Wouldn't need nothin' else in no stew with you," Cleo said to me. Except for the few times when she was blinded by prejudice, she was always first to perceive and mollify hurt feelings.

"How come you a teacher?" Uncle Wiggly, oblivious to Cleo's glare. His question was kindly meant.

"Woke up one morning with a terrible itch. Turned out to be the teaching itch, so I've been scratching and teaching ever since." What I had meant to be light had turned out to be heavy and dull, but Uncle Wiggly was not put off. He was used to forgiving dullness in adults.

"You *like* goin' to school?"

"Sometimes."

"You like goin' to our school?"

"No." Their silence invited me to say more, but I wanted a sign before taking the wrong direction.

"Then why you keep comin' back?"

"Keep hopin' it'll change, I guess."

"Hopin' never changed nothin'," Wentworth said. He had been quieter than usual, but now he was so emphatic that we all turned to look at him. "*Hope* this school gonna fall down but it don't. It stand right here, ever' mornin', ugly and mean."

"Too *gross* to fall down." Uncle Wiggly had used their favorite word. Wherever they had found it, they found a treasure; for them it summed all that was stupid, mean, and ugly into a single syllable.

"Gross," echoed Wentworth. "Grossest place in the whole world."

I meant to distract them with my question: "You want to do something about changing it?"

"Do Wentworth want a Cadillac?" Cleo, a quicker mind at fourteen than most of us at any age. It was the question she had been waiting for. She had been leaning forward, resting her chin in her hands; I watched her sit up and fold her hands in her lap. She was prepared to do business.

"Let me tell you why I come down here every week. Then we can talk about changing the school."

"Tell us iff'n you wants," replied Cleo. "We done already read that little blue book."

I have never been so disconcerted by a child's direct response. "That little blue book," a pamphlet written by me and published by the University of Michigan, described the penal school program called "English In Every Classroom" which I was struggling to transfer into public school practice. That little blue book had been imported into Garnet-Patterson in August of 1965 when I first distributed a copy to each teacher. If the faculty agreed upon anything, it was that those booklets should be kept from their students. As one teacher informed me, children resent learning things that are taught in reform school. She neglected to add that they could not possibly resent it as much as some of their teachers resent teaching things that are taught in reform school.

"*All* of you?" I asked, foolishly. I was astounded. Later I would realize that my astonishment grew from disbelief in their literacy. I did not believe they could have read that pamphlet.

"Sure. *Ever'*body want to know what you doin' here."

It was so reasonable if you were willing to credit them with normal sensibilities. You have a friend, you naturally want to know what he does with himself. If he doesn't know about Neptune, you find out for him. If he writes a little blue book, you read it.

"But how did you get the book? I mean. . . ." It was a stupid question. Did I want them to admit they had pilfered it? In one copy or five? I tried to retrieve my error. "I mean, I'm glad you read it."

"Anyway, we read it. You gonna tell us what we kin do?"

And that's how it began. In one way it started with Wentworth's magazine, with the Cadillac and trip to the airport, our visit to District News, a mounted policeman in front of the National Gallery. We made a number of beginnings in the last four months of 1965, but we did not begin our campaign until a Thursday in January when we sat together on the school steps in an unseasonably warm and weakening light.

We talked until the street was dark and cars were turning on their headlights as they passed. I explained the theory and operation of the program; they in turn told me where it was working in their classes and where it wasn't. In writing now about that first exchange of confidence and act of mutual recruitment, I realize how much their previous discretion made the conversation possible. Except for Snapper's reluctant revelation about the teacher who called names, and Wentworth's explicit feelings about his English teacher, none of the children had revealed to me their opinions of individual teachers and I had never asked. They had said much in general but little about particular teachers. Even now, with reason and invitation to talk about individuals, they preferred first to talk about ideas:

"If *ever'* teacher teach readin' and writin', some a them dumbheads still ain't gonna learn."

"He ain't worried none about them. He aimin' to get all the ones just *sits* there."

"Can't make a smarthead out of a dumbhead no way."

"Throw away them books, you see who's a dumbhead."

"Iff'n I could put my magazine on 'at desk, it sure be easier on my eyes." That was Wentworth's way of cooling the conversation. Any reference to the way I'd gotten to know him was usually good for a laugh.

I couldn't repeat all of that conversation even if I had full notes instead of a few words and memories in front of me. Four children actively argued the merits and deficiencies of a plan for teaching literacy, while a fifth echoed whoever was most vociferous and made occasional contributions of his own. My sense of reality, already diminished by Cleo's matter-of-fact statement that all five of them had read the booklet called "Teaching English At Boys Training

School," was further weakened by evidence that they had not only read it but understood it.

"Rubbergut in a dumbhead class," said Snapper. "He ain't never gonna be president, but he ain't never gonna be nothin' in that class." I had never heard Snapper talk with sympathy much less compassion about Rubbergut. Our conversation had turned to identifying teachers who were using the newspaper, pretending to use the newspaper, and not even bothering to do that. For the first time I had a clear picture of the inverted pyramid of privilege within the school:

Not only did children like Rubbergut get classroom wardens of whom nothing but discipline was expected, but those wardens would use only ancient textbooks to which they were well accustomed. The best got better and the worst got nothing. The truth could evoke pity even in a Snapper, even for a Rubbergut.

Perversity—brutal stupidity or willful ignorance, the difference doesn't matter; when found in teachers, damage done to children is the same—perversity can know no further refinement than refusal by three teachers (none of whom was candid about it beyond the classroom) to use the newspaper because of typographic errors in the bulldog edition. All three taught a majority of "donkey classes" (a common phrase in teachers' mouths, well-known and hated by children to whom it is applied) and all three had explained to their classes the corrupting effects of reading so imperfect a text as the *Post* provided. Better a pure ignorance than a sullied knowledge, and devil take the hindmost.

It was the hindmost who hit upon our first tactic. Rubbergut could eat any amount of almost anything, hence his name. But one thing he could not stomach was the pile of newspapers which lay untouched each day in the back corner of his English classroom. Rubbergut liked to read; he was quick to admit that he didn't understand some things, but he would rather read a good adventure story than do anything else. And he liked the newspaper, especially the comics and "numbers pages."

"The what?" I asked when he first told me his preferences. The question was merely a comment on the name, because I knew he must mean the sports pages. What I knew, however, was not what he meant; numbers that fascinated me in box scores and performance statistics were of small interest to Rubbergut when compared with numbers in beautifully ordered ranks and columns found on financial pages. Rubbergut was hooked on the stock market.

No, he didn't understand much of what he read on those pages; no, he wasn't simpleminded. What we define by utility he had redefined by beauty. Perhaps we are the simple ones, we who see only financial gains and losses in stock market reports of daily newspapers. When Rubbergut looked at those same pages he saw an endless riches of number symbolizing all the perfect complexity he knew the world must hold. For me, understanding how he felt was not easy; for him, explaining what he really wanted to know about the numbers was even more difficult, for their denotation interested him least. When you put them all together, he would ask, what do they mean? How could I explain that they mean a financial system, a nation, a way of life. . . . Eventually I settled for a beginning in simple meaning. It wasn't much of a beginning, for my little knowledge was a poor thing compared with his large imagination.

Rubbergut's tactical approach was masterful: *All* the boys and girls in his class were his friends; he would speak to each of them, and they would *all* demand the newspaper every day. He had tried it himself and gotten nowhere. His opinion was that his teacher could ignore him, but she wouldn't find it easy to ignore thirty like him. Worse came to worse, they could always *take* the newspaper and let her see what she could do about it.

There was quick agreement in the gang. Their only modification of Rubbergut's plan was in its extent. They would begin by recruiting a few of their friends instead of entire classes. All were agreed that the item to begin with was the newspaper and the place to begin was the classroom of every teacher who refused to use it. During their discussion of tactics, I discovered that they knew what my friend had said in the faculty meeting. He was speaking truth, they said, and it had made a difference. Rubbergut's report of the difference it made in his dumbhead English class struck the right note for ending a long afternoon:

The day after my friend publicly unburdened himself of the truth about teachers and newspapers, Rubbergut's English teacher instituted a new practice in her last class of the day. About ten minutes before the end of the hour, she distributed her pile of untouched newspapers and instructed her class to page rapidly through several different sections to answer several insignificant questions and "never mind being careful about the newspaper because it's going to be thrown away anyhow." Which was certainly an effective way of giving your newspapers that used look so valuable for preventing criticism by a fellow teacher whose boys collected them after school.

14

WE HAD KNOWN good times before, but never a better time than the Friday that followed our long conversation. Perhaps it was due to feelings of mutual satisfaction at working together to accomplish something that mattered. Perhaps it was because the unseasonably fine weather held for another day and the children, prepared by reading and expectation, were pleased by their visit to the Maryland campus. Or it was simply because they had dressed up to dine out. Whatever the reason, the day was a good one for all of us.

We had agreed to walk the campus until dark, which was early on those short midwinter days, and then to have supper at one of the College Park restaurants. My companions were excited by the idea of supper out, but Cleo surprised me by turning to Wentworth and asking a question in a phrase I hadn't heard since my Baltimore adolescence:

"How we holdin'?"

"Mor'n fi' dollars."

"We could stay out for eatin' iff'n you got the time," she said to me. This was the first I knew of their treasury, for I had only seen them make individual purchases of gum and candy. Once more their self-dependence and their dignity had put me to shame. In assuming that I would pay and that they would expect me to, I had again undervalued them. My training as a teacher was hard to overcome.

If our visit to the university campus appears to be part of a planned effort to expose children to better things in life (mine), then appearance is partly deceiving. I had no plan then, nor would I know how to make one now. The places we went together were places that had given me pleasure; because they pleased me, I thought they were likely to please them. In that, as in little else, I was almost always right. Part of the truth, I understand now in retrospect, is that they wanted to like what I liked and were determined to do so even at some cost to themselves. But that has little to do with our afternoon and evening in College Park.

That Friday was unusually busy both for me and for the children. With the end of the semester near, they were taken up with tests and I was occupied with preparations for new materials. As a result, I did not see any of them until we met after school. They were waiting for me as I came out of the building; when I saw them, I knew how good a day I wanted it to be. They had, for the first time, dressed up for the occasion.

Cleo looked years older in a sweater and skirt, a bright scarf tied at her neck; Snapper, Rubbergut, and Uncle Wiggly managed to look even younger than usual in white shirts and ties worn under their winter coats. But the most remarkable change was in Wentworth, who wore a sport jacket over a turtleneck sweater and carried a raincoat. The small-brimmed hat on his head completed the picture of a poised young man dressed for a social engagement. Where was the child who endured his English class by pretending illiteracy? Creating a truculent child out of an easy young man requires all the skill that schools can muster.

"Sweet threads," I said, brushing an imaginary speck from his lapel.

"Gonna make the big scene," he replied, blushing with pleasure.

"Looka them," Cleo said, moving her head toward the three smaller boys. "Ain't they somethin'?" She was balancing compliments for her boys; notice one, notice all. I commented on bright ties, polished shoes, creased pants—they had all done themselves proud. Cleo and Wentworth looked so mature and self-possessed that for the first time I did not think of them as children. To be taking them to a college campus seemed a fitting way to spend that Friday afternoon.

Today was Uncle Wiggly's turn to navigate. In spite of expert opinion, I had not believed that thirteen- and fourteen-year-old children could know so little about their geographical environment. Expert opinion, however, is occasionally right; though each of them had been in District schools since the first grade, they knew almost nothing about Washington. I do not believe, however, that their ignorance can be attributed solely or even significantly to inadequate schools. It has another dimension far less tangible and far more difficult to remediate.

That other dimension is identified in a story told me by an assistant superintendent of schools in Washington who once accompanied a kindergarten class on their first bus tour of the city. One stop on the tour was the Washington Monument, especially imposing on a hot, cloudless day. Sitting near the front of the bus, the assistant superintendent got off first so that he might help children down the high steps. After several had dismounted, one small boy stopped on the lower step and squinted up at the great white obelisk. He looked for a long moment, then shook his head and said —all five years of him, quietly, no question in his voice— "Ain't this a white man's world."

When I was an American soldier in Germany, I lived in a barracks full of college graduates who had been recruited into the Counter-Intelligence Corps. Many of them never saw any more of Germany than the local beer hall. Being vocal by training as well as introspective by nature, they talked about their strange immobility and lack of curiosity. Their conclusion, common to all even when arrived at in uncommon ways, was that they felt so much the unwanted aliens that discomfort overwhelmed education. A large number of intelligent, sensitive men saw Germany for a year through the bottom of a beer stein.

The black and impoverished child's beer hall is his neighborhood. Bad as it may be, it is his and he feels safer there —even with speed freaks and winos and child molesters— than he does in the alien white man's territory. Put him on a bus, run him through that territory, and the most probable accomplishment will be to intensify rather than lessen his alienation. In a world bounded by the barriers of his neighborhood, he may learn nothing; beyond those barriers, he may learn the full meaning of hopelessness and defeat.

Is this an argument against school programs which aim to "enrich" the child's experience? It is, if those programs are independent of the work, food, and housing by which a human being knows himself to be a creature worth regarding; it is, if they are independent of the home, family, and hope by which a child knows himself to be a creature worth enriching. The argument that "you have to begin somewhere" is pernicious in its implication that one beginning place may be as good as another, that a beginning must be made where resource and opportunity dictate.

But because I have little hope that those who have been improved can refrain from attempting to elevate the unimproved, my argument aims at change in tactics rather than revision of strategy. We must admit, I think, that we are dealing with an experience whose effect upon impoverished children can theoretically be measured upon either a positive or negative scale. We seem to have operated upon the belief that an "enrichment experience" can be something or nothing, but it cannot be less than nothing. It is time we recognized that it can be much less than nothing, that what civilizes us can savage an unprotected child. If we cannot resist the urge to improve and enrich, then we must also accept responsibility for protecting the children who satisfy our urges.

Preparation is a form of protection. On one of my journeys from Washington to Baltimore I spent several hours in College Park scouring the University of Maryland campus for illustrated brochures from various schools and colleges, and I purchased a book with excellent photographs of the campus, its environs, and its inhabitants. All this I gave to Cleo two weeks before our proposed visit, together with a large scale map of the District and its Maryland suburbs. She would distribute the materials so that everyone saw them, and she would appoint a navigator for the trip; we would meet during the following week to talk about the journey and the campus.

Not only did they read both brochures and book, but all five of them studied the map as well. After an hour's conversation that included some interesting questions about reality in the illustrations (did anybody really dress up like that just for going to school?), they spread out the map and showed me the route they had chosen. Though they had cooperated in selecting the route, Uncle Wiggly would be responsible for navigation.

"Go on. Show 'im," Cleo said to Uncle Wiggly.

"Aw naw. Nex' week." He was embarrassed, but his hand had gone into his pocket.

"Go on, man. Let 'im see it now." Snapper couldn't bear to postpone anything.

The hand came out of the pocket holding a World War II

United States Army compass. Having gotten lost several times with the help of similar ones, I recognized it while it was still grasped tightly in Uncle Wiggly's small fingers. The navigator was unquestionably prepared.

Not only was the navigator prepared, but so were his crew of four. The cultural shock of a white obelisk upon an unprotected black five-year-old may differ in degree from the cultural shock of a white university campus upon unprepared black adolescents. It may differ in degree, almost surely it will differ in the apparent response it provokes, but it does not differ in kind. I believe that all children must know about the institutions that shape the life of their country in order to know about themselves. But I also believe that the price of "exposure" (a favorite word of enrichers, who do not seem to realize that it can describe a fatal condition) can be the spirit of a child. No amount of enrichment can be worth the price.

The revolving responsibility for navigation had been Cleo's idea; the map had been mine, prompted by a map of Washington and its suburbs found by Wentworth in the glove compartment of a rented car. After some tentative probing on his part and mine, he admitted that he had never seen a map of Washington before and that he would like to find the street and block where he lived. Once he had confessed his ignorance and his interest, admission was easier for the others.

On that occasion the map provided a new and absorbing experience for all five of them. Subsequently, Cleo appointed a map-reader for each of our planned trips, Hertz supplied each child with a map of his own, and the children's expanding curiosity did the rest. In the process, the gang discovered that it possessed an unexpected talent.

Cleo and Wentworth had been competent navigators, but Snapper was superb. When his turn came, he traced the route to Arlington National Cemetery on six thin sheets of paper, colored each street differently, and included a scale for distance with an estimation of mileage between school and cemetery. Then to each of us he gave one of the sheets pasted onto a piece of sturdy drawing paper folded in thirds, with our names, the date, and his name on the outside. We were all impressed; Snapper's opinion, delivered with a depreciatory wave of his hand, was that it was "hardly nothing." We should wait till next time, when he would really show us something

15

UNCLE WIGGLY was nervous because he was navigating, but the other four were unusually subdued. Clothes do sometimes make the man; in this case, clothes were making men and a woman out of three boys and a girl. Not only did they sit as stiffly as adults instead of as comfortably as children, but even their voices seemed collared and creased. Our journey was decorous, our conversation dull.

We were halfway out Rhode Island Avenue before the stuffiness dissolved in a loud sigh by Rubbergut. I watched in the rearview mirror as he closed his eyes and sighed again. Snapper, sitting next to him, dug a warning elbow into his ribs.

"Can't help it, man. This here shirt gon' kill me dead." Rubbergut was tugging at the collar with his finger.

"Same shirt I got on. You don't hear me makin' no noise."

"Fit you. Don't fit me *no* way." Rubbergut was considerably heavier than Snapper; the shirt which had looked so well under his coat when he was standing, now appeared to be strangling him while he sat. With his talent for bulging his eyes and puffing his cheeks, he looked like the end was near.

"Loosen up on 'at collar 'fore you pops a button." Cleo's advice brought another deep sigh, this time of relief, as Rubbergut followed directions. Uncle Wiggly was already fumbling at his collar, his eyes shuttling from map to street signs, while Wentworth quietly removed his hat and unbuttoned his sport jacket. Only Snapper and Cleo didn't join the general easing, Cleo because she had nothing to loosen and Snapper because he would have lost face. For the moment at least, he preferred to lose air.

Uncorseted, the children relaxed and began to anticipate the visit. Their conversation touched several topics before it settled upon the area they found least comprehensible in the entire subject of colleges and campuses: people going to school even though no law said they had to. We had talked about it before, but they returned to it at the first opportunity. From their point of view, it was the most mystifying human action they had ever heard of.

At the beginning of the year, only the two ninth graders had any notion of what they would do when they could choose freely. Next year both would go on to high school, but for very different reasons. Cleo would go because she wanted to be a medical secretary, which a friend had told her required a high school diploma; Wentworth would go because his mother wouldn't let him leave school until he was sixteen. But neither had any intention of remaining in school one day longer than immediate goals demanded. Pretty pictures in a book or no pretty pictures, a school was a school; anybody who stayed longer than he had to was crazy. Did the mommas and poppas of all those people who went to college *make* them go? Yes, I answered, a great many of them did.

"People think they dumbheads iff'n they don't?"

"Naw, the kids, iff'n *they* don't go."

"Sure they dumbheads. Git the chance to go, you bet I be gone." Still buttoned up, sitting erect as a man with a neck brace, Snapper was indignant at Cleo's question. How to reconcile the pettish dullard of the classroom with the eager, ambitious child of our journeys and conversations? Could any public and recurrent experience be so bad that a child would develop protective schizophrenia to meet it? It could be; it is; children do. We have not begun to understand the pain we inflict nor the rage we engender with our merciless battering upon the fortress of the child's identity. Because its walls are so easily breeched, we treat its contents as negligible. Snapper's outer walls had long since been leveled and pulverized, but in an unfound place he maintained himself and his hope.

"You the dumbhead! You ain't gettin' no chance." Said loudly, emphatically; all the more remarkable because it was said by Wentworth, who was seldom mean or angry. He had turned in his seat to stare Snapper down.

"Get it iff'n I wants it." Snapper was surprised by Wentworth's outburst. He slid down in his seat as far as his tight collar would allow, and dropped his gaze to the seat in front of him.

"Who? The parents, if they don't make the kids go?"

"Shi-i. . . ." Wentworth had himself in hand. He turned back again to examine the dashboard, his eyes shielded and his face set.

"Why you wanna say that? Don' cost you nothin' iff'n I wants to go." Snapper, plaintively. The tone was so odd in his mouth that I looked back to see who was speaking.

"You a dumbhead." Wentworth, almost without emphasis.

"Actin' ain't bein'. Look on you."

"Gonna do it diff'runt, but ain't goin' to no college."

Going to do it different. Realizing what we had heard,

Cleo and I both turned to look at Wentworth who was now staring out the side window. Even with hat off and sport coat unbuttoned, he looked no part a child. He had won the battle with himself that he had been fighting all semester long. Wentworth was tired of hiding. He couldn't talk about it yet, or even bear to hear it talked about by someone else, but he had decided to abandon his cover.

16

LATE AFTERNOON traffic was pouring out of the campus as we approached it from the south. Though the time was only four o'clock, lines of cars waiting to enter or cross old Baltimore Pike gave the appearance of an entire university just released from a three o'clock class. As we stopped for a light before turning into the campus, an ancient fire truck swept across the boulevard in front of us. Its gleaming red body was as bright as the day it went into service, but its original equipment had been replaced with smiling, waving, windblown Maryland undergraduates of both sexes. Though fraternity letters painted on its side told me enough about it, they told my companions nothing.

"Looka them! Looka them!" Uncle Wiggly was about to burst. He had uttered nothing but monosyllables and short phrases containing driving instructions ever since we had left Tenth Street. The end of his responsibility that came with the campus in sight, coupled with the extraordinary apparition of that fire engine, was more than he could tolerate. He bounced in his seat, applauding and whistling as the truck full of undergraduates rolled past.

"How's that for something different?" I spoke to Cleo as Uncle Wiggly subsided when the fire truck entered a side road and passed from sight.

"Wasn't 'zactly what I was lookin' for."

"No, I guess not. Sort of surprised me too."

"You seen 'at black girl?"

I had, and wondered if she had. "I saw her. Surprise you as much as the fire engine?"

Sitting beside me, she turned to look directly at me. "Pretty good. Surprise me pretty good."

In all those white students attached in various ways and places to that fire engine, the one black girl had been especially conspicuous. At the University of Maryland in the 1965–66 academic year, black students were conspicuous both by their mass absence and their individual presence. I had been surprised to see a black girl on that fire engine; Cleo's instincts had brought her the same reaction.

"Teachers nigger on you here?" We had come a longer way than the few miles from Tenth Street to College Park. Snapper had asked the question without thinking about his language; Cleo was waiting for my answer without reacting to it. I chose my words as carefully as I could.

"Never to your face. And most of them will never think it. But some will. There's always a few."

"Here same as any other place."

"No, it's different. People here do a lot of thinking. You can't think and use words like *spic* and *dago* and *kike* and *honkey* and *nigger*." None of them, I discovered, knew what a *spic* or a *dago* was; only Cleo and Wentworth had heard *kike* before. Snapper wanted to know why I put in *honkey*.

"Why not?" I answered. "What makes it different from *nigger*?"

"It don't hurt no honkey."

I had to admit that he had a point. Still, I said, it was meant to hurt. That counts, too.

"Don't count as much as *nigger*."

Maybe not with the person who hears it, I said, but it counts with the person who uses it.

"Sure do." Cleo brought the subject to a close as we parked in a visitors' parking lot: "You be honkeyin' people, they be niggerin' you."

During a warm, damp, winter's afternoon, the University of Maryland occasionally enjoys a spring-like mist that seems to rise from the acres of green grass that are the campus's chief adornment. At such times the Georgian red-brick architecture is much softened at its sharp edges and the mist-muted sounds of voices have a less immediate and intrusive effect. Even automobile traffic that surrounds the campus with coils of fumes and harsh noises, is altered in its nervous nature to something slow-moving and placid. Except perhaps for a fine evening in early summer, no time is more pleasant for a visit to the University. For two hours, until full dark, we wandered over the campus and through its buildings.

"They sure enough got the vines."

"Lookit him. Ain't he somethin'?"

The clothes (vines) were more or less as brochures had promised. In January of 1966 the University of Maryland may not have been overburdened with serious students, but it had more than its share of dedicated dressers. Because my three visits since winter and spring of that year have been confined to late afternoon or evening lectures for graduate and professional groups, I do not know whether well turned-out has given way to well turned-on in undergraduate Maryland sartoriality. But I do know that the greatest deviation we saw that day was a stylish young lady carrying her handsome shoes and pensively walking barefoot in the grass.

The hours between four and six are the best visiting hours on a college campus. With most of the day's activities done and most of the people gone, grounds and buildings are usually open and inviting. When darkness comes, either classes resume or buildings are locked; with failing light, the campus closes in and the sense of welcome is gone. Perhaps that was the best part of our visit: The children felt welcome and responded with openness and warmth.

We wandered through a laboratory building; a graduate student took us into one of the labs and explained the uses of some exotic equipment. When we left, Wentworth asked me if I understood about that kind of stuff.

"No," I said, which was the truth. Zoology and chemistry almost finished my college career soon after it began.

"Didn't think so," he said, with a smile. "You wasn't lookin' while he was talkin'." They miss so little; we offer them less.

"He know plenty 'bout English." Snapper had never defended me before. Usually that was Cleo's self-appointed task, but she had heard Wentworth's kindly tone while Snapper had not.

"Sure he do," said Wentworth, gently. I decided that our next stop would be the library, where I had an edge. I felt as though I needed one.

At that hour the library was nearly empty, yet it offered us a sight we had not seen before on campus. The girl on the fire truck was the only black to cross our path until we entered the library and discovered five boys and girls studying together at a table. We had not seen a great many people of any description in the hour before we visited the library, but the several hundred we encountered were unmistakably white. The only reaction this provoked had been Snapper's caustic aside to Cleo's observation that it would be coming on for dark pretty soon.

"Yeah," he said, "and then it be the only other dark thing here."

We stood in the entranceway, looking into the large reading room. Though there was much to see, I knew that five pairs of eyes were fixed on five dark faces at a nearby table. The children were as motionless as I, but something nameless bespoke our presence to one of the boys sitting at the table. He turned to look at us, looked long, then whispered to the girl sitting next to him. She looked, then both rose from their chairs and came toward us. Uncle Wiggly actually stepped back two paces as he watched them approach.

"Hello," the boy said. "Can we help you?" The question was addressed to me, but managed to include my companions as well. Though the boy asked it, the expression on the girl's face said that he was speaking for both of them.

"You've already helped us," I answered. "In a big place like this it helps to have somebody say hello."

"It is a big place," the boy said, "and it looks even bigger when it's empty. Almost everybody has left for supper." He was very easy. I could feel the children relax; Uncle Wiggly took a tentative step forward.

"Have you ever been here before?" the girl asked. Her question had been undirected, but I took it up because I didn't want the children put at a disadvantage.

"On the campus?" I asked. "Yes. Often. But my friends are visiting with me for the first time and we're trying to see as much as we can before dinner. I've only used the library once, so I really don't know it very well."

"*We* know a lot about it," said the girl, laughing. "Don't we, Rob?"

"The five of us meet here every day to study together," Rob explained. "It's about the only quiet place with good lights where you can study with your friends. And it's got all the books for our courses."

"Could we show you around a little?" the girl asked "We're about finished studying anyway."

They didn't show us a little; they showed us everything, and they showed it well. When we'd had our tour, they took us back to their table and introduced us to two girls and a boy we hadn't met. Because we were all tired of walking, and because the library was almost empty, we sat together and talked.

"I know Garnet-Patterson," George, the other boy, said when he found out where we were from. He told us that he had gone to high school in the District after his father had taken a job with the government and moved his family from Newark. George had a friend who had gone to Cardozo High School, just three or four blocks from Garnet-Patterson, and this friend had a younger sister who had been in the junior high school. Having traced George's connection with the school, we now had to trace the gang's connection with George. Sure enough, Cleo knew the younger sister he was talking about, and Wentworth thought maybe his older cousin had gone with her for a while. Had we the time, we would certainly have discovered relationships beyond number and belief.

While they harrowed common ground, I was able to sit back and watch them. No one, watching or listening, could possibly have known that my companions were three followers, a lieutenant, and a leader. Cleo was artful in drawing out her boys, at the same time appearing to be no more than one amongst equals. But it was she who led the conversation from who knew what and whom to who knew a good place for us to eat dinner. Because I was tired and warm from walking, and the library was heated by calendar instead of thermometer, I was relaxed and a little drowsy until I suddenly realized what I was hearing:

"That a good place for *us*?"

"It's all right," answered Rob. "You'll be all right there."

"You mean there are places around here where we

wouldn't be?" I had spoken to Rob, but Dora—the girl who had greeted us with him—answered me.

"Well, you know, nobody ever *says* saything, or almost nobody, but it's there. So we just don't go to those places. There are a lot of good places so it doesn't matter."

"Anyway, *you'd* be alright. *You* could go." The tone was edged and nasty, the speaker a girl who had said very little. There was no mistaking her intention.

"We together. We goes with him." Cleo was no longer one of five. She was the leader and everybody at the table knew it. Her voice had been so flat and uncompromising that the other girl actually pulled back from the table. It was a voice and a manner that demanded care. Except for the girl she had answered, the others looked at her with new interest.

So did I, but for a very different reason. This time I was certain I had heard what once before I had suspected. While I had been relaxed and a bit drowsy, I had heard Cleo speaking standard American English. The change hadn't struck me until I heard her lapse into the black argot which she always spoke in my presence: "*We* together. We *goes* with him." And minutes before I had heard her say, "*We're* in the ninth grade" when speaking of herself and Wentworth, and "We *go* to Garnet-Patterson" when asked where she and the boys went to school. For the first time I understood that she was operating on a double language standard, and that *at least in part she knew it.*

Cleo's several tongues are tangible clues to a language phenomenon which, when understood, is vital to the education of a small but disproportionately important group of children. This group was once part of a much larger class populated by children of immigrant Americans who spoke a tongue other than English in home and neighborhood. These children learned standard English because it was taught in the schools, it was spoken in the exterior community into which they ventured as they grew older, and *because their parents wanted them to*. Only one of these powerful reasons for learning standard English has any significance for today's equivalent group, now composed primarily of blacks, Spanish-Americans, and rural Southern whites.

One of these three motivating forces still retains some modest effect because standard English remains the language of pedagogy. What has greatly changed, however, is the incidence of real intercourse between this group and the exterior community, and the attitude of the interior community toward the standard tongue. By *real* intercourse I mean neither exposure to television nor physical time spent outside the language neighborhood. Ghetto children regard the language of television as part of the life of television—both belong to somebody else. The language of television, in their view, no more reflects a real life than does the language of the schools. That both happen to be the same language only confirms their belief.

The same unreality erodes the ground upon which verbal intercourse between communities is usually built. A child or a man learns to perform in a certain way because he wants to or because he must. In the case of a child who speaks nonstandard English, his motivation for learning the standard tongue of an exterior community is greatly diminished by his sense that the language of that community will be of little use to him in obtaining its privileges. Children of white immigrants knew they had only to assume the clothing of the dominant group—in large part, its language— and they could live undetected in its midst. Knowing that lifelong masquerade to be beyond them—being so informed by the shape of everything from the obelisk of the Washington Monument to the rectangle of a television box—

black and brown children see no reason for wearing clothes that give them neither warmth nor camouflage.

The diminished incidence of real intercourse between these interior and exterior language communities, while a formidable fact in itself, has small force for children independent of the attitude of their parents toward that community and its language. Not only did immigrant communities covet the position and privilege of the dominant group, they coveted the trappings of that privilege as well. To live like *them* was not only to dress and eat and spend like them, it was also to speak like them. Countless thousands of middle-aged adults today can tell poignant stories of grandparents forbidden to speak the old tongue to their grandchildren because parents wanted children to be Americans. To be American was to speak American, was to be free of the past. Today, for the child whose skin color is deeper than certain shades of pink or olive, to be American and speak American is not to be free of that past at all. Parents, knowing this, see little reason to learn the standard tongue, either for their children or for themselves. Or, far worse, they actively reject that tongue for themselves and for their children *because* of its association with a repressive past and present.

This attitude of the parents, which effectively places the ghetto school in an adversary culture, not only serves to counteract intercourse with speakers of the dominant tongue, but also serves to negate the historical value of language spoken and taught in the schools. With this negation, the positive value of standard English as the language of pedagogy is largely lost to the ghetto child.

All this is to treat generally of many impoverished children. Great numbers of such children cannot speak standard English and do not want to learn to speak it. For them, alternative teaching methods and materials will never be enough; the fault lies in society and cannot be remedied solely by the schools. This is not to absolve the schools from responsibility for participating in that remediation. It is, however, to insist (as schools must insist) that in this instance they cannot be expected to accomplish themselves what other institutions and individuals cannot or will not do. And it is to state without qualification that most children will not learn in school what their family and community do not value outside of school.

To treat generally of impoverished children is by no means to speak of all. My experience with Cleo led me to search for and discover a significant number of children who, having mastered both a dialect and a standard tongue, consciously repress the standard tongue. This remarkable act is exactly opposed to the far older American practice of learning both and consciously repressing the dialect. This new repression is an index to the damaged faith of the individual who learns and to the moribund doctrine of the institution which teaches.

Just as the most important assumption of the program called "English In Every Classroom" is that most adolescent nonreaders are children who won't read rather than children who can't read, so the most important assumption about the language of many bright but impoverished black or brown children is that they speak as they do through choice and not through ignorance. Their choice is neither hasty nor capricious; they are the ones who truly "know better" when they follow the language pattern of their dialect. What they may also know better is what's better for them, just as Wentworth knew what was better for him when he chose feigned illiteracy as his protection against the indignities of school. They know that standard English isn't worth its cost; they know that they may not be able to prevent their minds from learning it, but they also know that they can prevent their mouths from speaking it. They know that it is better repressed because it has no place in their lives. Who but a fool practices for a contest to which he will not be admitted, a struggle in which he will not be allowed to compete?

The successful education of such children, especially in the middle grades, may depend entirely upon convincing them that they can satisfy the criteria for admission and compete in the contest with the right kind of preparation. What this means is that grammatical and rhetorical remediation for many bright children may be as foolish as reading remediation for unwilling readers. Neither needs a patching and bandaging of intellect; both need repair of motive, a reason to change the attitude which expects, invites, and bitterly welcomes defeat. No such reason can be found entirely within the ghetto, but no such reason can be made acceptable or persuasive outside the ghetto unless it takes fully into account the dignity and integrity of the child. In the case of very bright children, at least, this means making them full participants in their own experience.

17

ROB, DORA, AND GEORGE walked across the campus with us; the unpleasant girl and her friend went elsewhere. Were I that girl, I would have gone elsewhere too. Though Cleo assumed a softer guise, she had exposed herself long enough for discovery. The three who remained with us liked what they had found; the other two obviously felt more comfortable somewhere else.

Rob's easiness was disarming, and he knew it. In the scant half hour between when the two girls left us and we parted with the remaining three, he managed to charm Cleo, speak seriously with every member of the gang but one, point out places on our campus route, and interrogate me about who I was and why I was with my companions. His performance was admirable, and I cooperated in every way but one.

The one access I denied him was to Wentworth. For the first time Wentworth needed my protection, because for the first time Cleo's imagination failed her. To the moment when she met Rob, I had never known her to be inadequate to the needs of her boys and herself. Inexperience counted for less with her than with any person I have known. For some people experience matters less because the shape of their ego matters more; they are the ones who remain largely unchanged by circumstance. For Cleo experience mattered greatly, but she had an unusual capacity for anticipating its demands by a previous effort of the imagination. Because Rob was an experience she had been unable to imagine, she was unprepared for him; he swept her along on the sweet tide of his talk and attention.

Everybody was having a good time except Wentworth. He had enjoyed the library tour and the easy exchange when we had returned to the table. But his pleasure turned sour from the moment Rob really noticed Cleo for the first time. For if Cleo had not anticipated the Robs of this world, Wentworth had always known them to exist. Here before him, packaged into one light brown skin, was all the competence he had just begun to recognize as his own chief desire. Bad enough to know that you don't have it, but worse to see it confirmed by tangible contrast. Worst of all, however, to see it confirmed by demonstration on your most valued possession.

Rob, Dora, and George had been an unexpected addition to our day. Even more unexpected was the problem their presence made for me: They were preparing to have dinner with us, and I didn't want that to happen. As we walked across the campus I watched Wentworth draw into himself until he reminded me more of the boy who sat dumbly in his English class than the young man who had faced and mastered the decision to "do it different." Finding Wentworth unresponsive to his overtures and finding me annoyingly in his way, Rob became more aggressive and open in his questions and opinions:

"You mean you fly here from Detroit *every* Thursday?'

"Every school Thursday, yes."

"Are there many white teachers at Garnet-Patterson?"

"Very few."

"Don't you think a black man would have an easier time doing what you're doing?"

"I'm sure of it."

I haven't reported the conversation as it actually happened. The questions are Rob's, the answers mine, and they did occur in this sequence. They did not, however, occur consecutively, for Rob divided himself amongst all of us even when concentrating on me. And he was far too clever to risk antagonizing Cleo again by a frontal assault on me. During the memorable hour we spent together, I came slowly to recognize him as an exceptionally well-disguised young militant who did not like the sight of a white man and five black youngsters together. That he had a right to his view I do not deny. That his view is right I do entirely deny, and I have done and shall continue to do all I can to prevent it from prevailing.

What I most wanted to do on that Friday evening was to prevent Rob and his companions from having supper with us. Empty of ideas for doing it by suggestion instead of by prescription, and doubting the power of suggestion in those circumstances, I had nearly determined to tell the three of them that we were grateful for their good company but we would like to have dinner by ourselves. I don't know how I would have said it, and I think it could have been a very unhappy experience. Fortunately, perhaps, I never had to say anything; Wentworth handled it for us all.

"I'm sure of it," I said, volunteering no information, interested in what his prejudice would do with my passive response. But Wentworth gave him no chance to do anything with it.

"He makin' the difference," Wentworth said. "Books and newspapers don't know nothin' 'bout his color."

"You don't understand . . . ," was as far as Rob got. Of all
the phrases he might have used, no other was so surely
guaranteed to antagonize Wentworth. How many thousand
times had he heard or felt the same words from similar
mouths?

"Understan' his color don't matter none. Don't need to
know nothin' else." Rob was a handsome, tall boy accustomed to domination; Wentworth was neither handsome
nor tall, more accustomed to submit than to dominate. He
hesitated, looked away, then took a step forward and spoke
directly to Rob: "Listen," he said, "we got to be goin' now.
You give us your telephone number, we get on to you nex'
time we here."

That's all there was to it, except for one event that
occurred six months after Rob had written his name,
address, and telephone number on a sheet of notebook paper
and given it to Wentworth. I don't know whether Cleo
understood what happened between Rob and Wentworth. I
know Snapper did, because I heard him say to Wentworth,
as we said good-bye and walked away toward the restaurant
where he would be all right, "Man, you really turn that cat
off!" It was clear to him, as it was to me, that Wentworth
was already doing things different.

Our meal was a great success, and to Wentworth belonged
the credit. He was masterful, he was entertaining, he was
never better. He had won a victory and he knew it. Never
before had he dominated his fellows or his surroundings as
he did that evening. How Cleo felt about her lieutenant
becoming captain-for-an-evening is difficult to say. She ate
as heartily as the rest, laughed as loudly at Wentworth's
jokes, contributed her share of comments and observations,
and never during the entire meal asserted her position of
leadership. She even left financial negotiations to Wentworth, who had always been at best a passive treasurer.

I knew that Wentworth's value had increased in his own eyes by his handling of Rob, but it required a series of acts on his part before I began to understand just what that successful confrontation meant to him. First of all, he refused to go into the restaurant Rob and his friends had selected for us. That place wasn't for us, he said. Solicitous of me, he enquired if I cared about how some people might feel about us eating together. He was so young and so earnest when he asked me the question that I could only shake my head. I intended to tell him he didn't have to ask me a question like that, but I realized in time to keep from hurting his feelings that he wasn't asking a question so much as he was performing a ritual. As leader of our group, he was responsible for the welfare of all its members.

Several restaurants were convenient to us; Wentworth consulted our desires, but he made the decision. When he broached the subject of finance to me, he did it with such maturity that I knew he had finally shed his constricting, childish skin:

"We got fi' dollars and fifty cents. Kin we eat in there for that much?"

"No."

"How much more we need?"

"Maybe three dollars."

They pooled their pocket cash and found three and a half dollars amongst them. Wentworth put it all together, carefully counted nine dollars, and put it in his pocket. We were walking toward the restaurant when he gave me the single greatest surprise of my entire relationship with the gang:

"Get a good meal in here for a dollar and a half?"

"Better one for a dollar-eighty," I said, correcting his faulty arithmetic.

He looked puzzled for a moment, then replied, "Well, guess we ain't got that much. Anyway, how come you know the price? Thought you say you ain't never eat here."

"Never have," I said. "I was just dividing five people into nine dollars."

"Who ain't gonna eat?" he asked, genuinely surprised. Then, looking around at each of us elaborately, "They sure six of us here, big as life."

I understood, and I blushed. I could feel my face get warm and I had to look away from those bright, frank eyes. I was being taken to dinner and I hadn't grace enough to anticipate their kindness.

"Come on," Wentworth said, taking my arm for a moment. "We gonna see what they givin' for a buck and a half."

For a buck and a half they gave a lot. If they didn't lose any money on their fish-in-a-basket Friday night special, they certainly didn't make any on us. Rubbergut outdid himself, and the rest of us were close behind. "All you can eat" is a phrase that needs careful application; applied indiscriminately to six large appetites, it can cause a waitress to shake her head in disbelief as she fills a basket for the fourth time. It can also lead to a problem which was solved by Wentworth's new *savoir faire*.

We had eaten and drunk to satiety. Rubbergut was barely breathing, though I had seen him wait until Snapper was looking elsewhere before loosening his pants. Uncle Wiggly was too full to twitch; even Wentworth's vivacity had been dulled beneath the weight of four baskets of fish and chips. I would gladly have loosened my belt, taken off my shoes, and lay down on the bench for a nap. But I knew we had a problem that had to be handled: "She's a good waitress," I said, to nobody. "We've worked her hard."

"Bet she be glad to see us gone," said Snapper. "She gon' have to charge old Rubbergut twice."

"Somebody gon' have to carry me to that car," Rubbergut replied from somewhere deep inside himself. He looked immobile as a statue of the Buddha.

"Well *she* ain't gonna do it," Snapper said, pointing to the passing waitress. "She done enough already."

"She has," I agreed. "You all about ready to go?" They were, so I approached the problem: "Look, you've taken me to dinner and I'm grateful. You've taken care of me, but how about the waitress? May I help take care of her?"

"I thought on that while we was eatin' and I figured sixty-six cents maybe wasn't enough." Wentworth paused, then looked directly at me when he spoke: "We'd be proud to have you help."

One dollar and thirty-nine cents per dinner times six dinners, subtracted from nine dollars, leaves sixty-six cents. I added a dollar, let the teacher in me explain that fifteen percent was considered fair payment for good service, got told by Cleo that fifteen percent of eight dollars and thirty-four cents weren't no dollar sixty-six, and followed five happy adolescents from the restaurant, leaving one exhausted waitress behind.

"How you figure percentage?" asked Rubbergut as we gathered on the sidewalk before starting back to our car. During our slow, relaxed walk across campus, Cleo taught Rubbergut (and several others, who tried to be casual about listening) a precise and illuminating lesson on the simple arithmetic of percentage. What Rubbergut had never been able to understand when associated with school, he understood completely when associated with food. As Snapper, who understood percentage, said—"Man can't figure fifteen percent can't eat in no restaurant." For Rubbergut, that was home truth.

When the lesson on percentage was done, our conversation was worn out. Had the path to our automobile not taken us past the library and had we not seen Dora entering, our silence might have remained unbroken until we returned to Washington. As it was, Dora did not see us and no one in the gang called to her as we walked past. But Rob was very much on Wentworth's mind, and Dora was reminder enough to jog his memory and his tongue: "Went to that restaurant an' *nobody* messed on us. What *she* know?"

We walked another twenty feet in silence before he had it worked out to his satisfaction. He stopped, and so did we. "Iff'n we'd of listened to them, we'd never of got them good fish and potatoes. Ever' time, you got to go see for youself." No one contradicted him, nor did anyone have more to say until College Park was far behind us. As we left the campus, I couldn't help but think that a good many university students didn't know what Wentworth had learned that evening.

18

RUBBERGUT FELL ASLEEP and snored gently all the way back to Tenth Street. Snapper elbowed him awake a few times, then gave up the unequal battle and joined him. Wentworth and Cleo alternated between sleep and drowsy wakefulness; only Uncle Wiggly was alert for the entire journey, and he was forced to it by his navigational responsibilities. I assured him I'd wake him if I got lost, but he would have none of that. As a result, we talked together uninterrupted by others for the first time since we met.

It was Uncle Wiggly who led me more fully to understand the impact of the University upon the children. His conversation divided itself into three parts, each reflecting an aspect of the experience which had deeply moved him. One I expected; the other two, both more important than the one I anticipated, revealed another world to me.

He began with a vivid recollection of "all that grass." He and his ma had walked clear around the White House because they had been so taken by that vast expanse of lawn. But it didn't look like grass that was meant for walking on. It was meant for looking, that much was clear to him, which reduced it considerably in his eyes. Like a butcher's shop he had once seen, window full of the biggest steaks anybody ever saw. Didn't even make him hungry, he told me, because seeing them cold in a window was one thing; seeing them hotted up on a plate was another. Same was true of the central campus at the University of Maryland. All that grass for *walking on*. It beat anything he'd ever seen.

One thing he wished he'd done. Do like that girl we'd seen—take off his shoes and walk barefoot in the grass. He wouldn't mind coming all the way back to do it. Wasn't that much walking grass anywhere he knew about.

For many reasons I had guessed that the children would be taken by the great expanse of grass on the Maryland campus. When you live within boundaries of street intersections which tie together tight bundles of grassless houses fronting concrete sidewalks and macadam streets, you become an admirer of grassland. Children and adults who have spent their lives walking on concrete pavements and concrete-hard earth, are people with a passion for the soft resiliency of grass.

The passion for grass is a transferable desire. It can be passed from generation to generation, from poor white to poor black, from penthouse inhabitant to basement dweller with undiminished strength. But other passions are not so portable, especially private desires like the two Uncle Wiggly talked about after his way had been eased by a slope of grass:

How those five looked, sitting and studying at the table. It wasn't just the big library, though that was something. What it was . . . and here he stopped to contemplate the scene in his imagination, to find right words for a new experience. . . . What it was, they had looked like they *belonged* there. They were *happy* about sitting at that table; he could see it on their faces.

We talked for many minutes about Rob and Dora and George and the other two girls. At first I was sure I understood what had impressed him. Simple interpretations were readily available to me: Don't all outsiders desire a place within the circle of those who belong? Coming in from a darkening white man's world, wouldn't lighted faces and dark skins make a memorable sight? All true, but only a background to Uncle Wiggly's delight.

As he talked I began to understand that he had been moved by an element in the scene which had escaped me completely. *He had never consciously seen a group of students happily studying together.* He had never even imagined it. His eyes had seen so much more than physical facts. Incredulously, he spoke of it now: Nobody there to make them do it. Wasn't nobody in that room and they could leave any time they wanted. But they stayed. They stayed because they wanted to, because they liked to. . . . For all Uncle Wiggly the Navigator knew or cared, I was enroute to Antarctica. The map lay unused on his knees as he stared at his memory of that implausible scene.

I should have guessed the third aspect of the day's experience that meant most to him. Once in my own life I had been continuously hungry for eighteen months. When anyone asks me what was the best summer of my life, I think of the July and August that followed hard upon those eighteen months and brought an end to my hunger. I can still remember many of the meals I ate during those wonderful two months. Though I think of it, I seldom speak of it as the best summer of my life because hunger is not a comfortable topic for an overfed people. Even for Uncle Wiggly it was awkward, though he too had knowledge of it from his own belly.

Uncle Wiggly had been so dumbfounded by the unlimited fish and chips that he had not been able to give it his best. He mourned the lost opportunity, for no one had ever before told him he could have as much as he wanted. Not that he hadn't had more than he could eat, but having more than enough is different from being told before you take the first bite that you can't eat too much *no matter how much you eat*. He wasn't complaining, mind, but if he ever got to the same place again he'd do it different. Next time he'd stick close to the fish and french fries; bread and greens and such could wait to see if he had room.

He said his words and phrases with large, intervening empty spaces, filling the gaps with an interior speculation that he kept hidden from me and the occasional attention of Cleo or Wentworth. Then he said something in so small a voice that I thought he must be speaking to Snapper or Rubbergut in the rear of the car. One glance in the mirror told me otherwise: The two of them were piled together in a corner of the seat, asleep. Another glance to my right at the two bobbing heads in front, and I knew he had to be talking either to me or to himself.

"I didn't hear what you said."

"Do Rob and them eat much as they want?"

"Yes."

"All the time?"

"Just about, I guess."

"You too?"

"Yes."

"Man. . . ."

There was no more to the conversation. It was as stark and brutal as any I have ever had with child or adult. Uncle Wiggly was a complex, intelligent thirteen-year-old boy who had never before considered the possibility that other black children or someone he knew well had all they wanted to eat most of the time. There was nothing simpleminded about him, but he never before had reason to look so long at the ugliest face of poverty—not the featureless impersonal mountain between nothing and everything, but the familiar face of the wall between too little and enough. Because I know of no way to ease the pain of that recognition, I did not try. We said no more for the rest of our journey.

19

THE SECOND SEMESTER began in a warm blaze of documented accomplishment and good feeling for many members of the faculty at Garnet-Patterson. Three events contributed to a general change in attitude, most apparent being the flood of materials which inundated library, bookroom, and classroom alike. With funding of current budgets for District governance, promised money became real money for purchase of paperbound books and magazines from District News Company. Money in hand, I was able to fulfill our needs without abusing Mr. Ottenstein's charity and good will. For the first time, we had materials enough to make the program a reality.

Appearance of our long-awaited materials did more than alter the look of the school; it altered its feeling as well. This change in feeling grew from parallel phenomena affecting students and faculty. For students, the phenomenon was one of justified belief: Most teachers had explained to their classes withdrawal of old texts and substitution of paperbound materials. Massive use of newspapers in many classes had been represented as introduction to promised magazines and paperbound books. Now promises were being redeemed, and we were reaping benefits from faith restored.

If faith was the phenomenon rewarded in students, its parallel was good works in teachers. Some who had worked to support the program in their own classrooms and to recruit colleagues in other classrooms, now found themselves with double success in hand. If magazines and paperbound books gave the program new scope for teachers who had leaned heavily on *The Washington Post*, it also gave them leverage with their reluctant colleagues. In the first week of the new semester we experienced a rush of converts nearly equal in number to those who had toiled in the vineyard since August and early September. It was a heady experience for all of us who had become resigned to battle lines drawn through the middle of the faculty.

New materials were everywhere, and so were results of tests given to students at the end of the first semester by a school psychologist whose assignment was evaluation of "English In Every Classroom." Using various measurements of verbal facility normally taken at the end of each school year, she discovered that children were learning at about twice their normal rate—*normal* defined as a child's average rate of learning determined by the same tests in previous years. Neither my colleagues nor I thought the tests highly significant since our primary aim was to change the children's feeling about literacy rather than their performance. We were glad to know that they were performing better, which might or might not be an indication of changed attitude, but the crucial question still remained whether they liked what they were doing.

That may have been the crucial question for us, but it was less important for both committed and uncommitted teachers. They had been too long trained in the old dogma of performance to be happy with a new dogma of feeling.

In this case the old dogma was a considerable ally. Talk all you want about attitude, many teachers told me; we'll agree that it would be pleasant if children liked to read and write. But pleasant as it might be, it is not necessary. What is necessary is that they satisfy certain standards of action. A good attitude is better than a bad attitude, but better than both is good performance. Nobody pays us or praises us for causing children to feel better about what they do.

Perhaps new materials and encouraging test results would have been enough to tip the balance. Perhaps, but I doubt it; I think tests and materials are likely to influence teachers with rational objections and reservations. I think them unlikely to influence those who object to change in any form and those who venerate their own educations. Though membership in both groups overlaps, it does not coincide. Together, however, the two memberships form a potent force for imposing past upon future and for discrediting present experience as unreliable. No force has been more responsible for damaging schoolchildren of all kinds, and less responsive to schoolchildren of the kind called impoverished.

A third event marked the beginning of the new semester. Taken together with paperbound materials and positive testing, it accounts for significant recruitment to the program during the second semester at Garnet-Patterson. The third event was Cleo and her boys. They were ingenious; they were enthusiastic; most of all, they were experienced and persistent. With little advice requested or offered, they learned to concentrate their efforts at two vulnerable points in the school's armor:

Recalcitrant teachers were first targets for the gang's careful aim. Since each was in a different class in two separate grades, they were able to attend to a large number of teachers themselves. Recidivists and holdouts earned their attention; where they lay beyond the children's own classes, dissatisfied friends were recruited to lengthen their reach. It was this selective recruitment which led to and became their second target.

Rubbergut had wanted to speak to all his classmates to gain their help in convincing uncooperative teachers that new materials were meant for every child in every classroom. His companions had rejected the idea because they thought they could handle the whole school with help from a few friends. They were right in their assumption but wrong in their belief that the campaign could be limited to a few frontline troops. I never knew how many children were involved, but I do know that Cleo and Wentworth became a clearinghouse for campaign information. It soon became an open secret amongst their fellows that they were leading an underground battle to keep newspapers, magazines, and paperbound books in use in every classroom. Their battle was remarkably successful.

During the end of February and beginning of March, the program in Garnet-Patterson moved from near failure to near success. If a third of the faculty was still uncooperative, and would remain so throughout my year of intense association with the school, another third doubled the size of the original group. During that period the children were very active, the river of paperbound materials was still rising within its banks, and the psychologist's postive test results were just becoming fully known in the school. For me, all efforts coalesced and came to have meaning in a memorable faculty meeting held on a Thursday afternoon early in March.

Before describing that uncommon meeting, however, I want to examine a more common attitude symptomatic of the most serious internal problem in American public education. That attitude is exemplified in adverse reaction to using children as levers to uproot ingrown teachers, a reaction which my account of the gang's work has sometimes brought from other educators. I have repeated parts of this story before a sufficient variety of teachers and school administrators to have learned what I did not know before: That such use of children is unethical practice to be avoided at any cost. Even at the cost of children's hope and education.

"Unethical" is an interesting word, implying as it does a code against which actions can be measured. In this case, one part of the code prohibits clandestine agreements between teachers and students because such agreements strike at the very heart of the teacher-student relationship. Put simply, that relationship is *us* and *them*; wherever that distinction is blurred, the code is violated and an unethical act has been committed.

The urge to write "us *against* them" is difficult to resist, for it is the most widespread corruption of the code and characterizes relationships of teachers to students in vast numbers of classes for unpromising children. This particular corruption is especially pernicious because it leads to protection of the system at the cost of the child. Again my desire is to write the more radical phrase, for I believe that the prevalent notion of "us against them" leads to protection of the system and *destruction* of the child.

My evidence is this: More often than I want to remember I have been asked a question which contains a thousand queries but implies only a single significant response. The question is—what can *I* do to make a real difference in the lives of these children, my students? The beginning of an answer is implied by the question: I do not do enough; I want to do more. Then the question becomes—what *more* can I do? Referring as it does to a spectrum of action, *more* also implies the ethical question: How much is too much?

To which the answer has almost always been the code response: "Too much" is action against the system; since one action against the system is to form a league with children, such an action is unethical.

Because I think the range of significant response to the question must be broadened, I now propose a restructuring of the code and a redefinition of the ethical concept which determines so much of the student-teacher relationship in school. First is the judgment of priority explicit in ordering the two groups. The customary phrase is "student-teacher," but in fact the phrase is more habitual than descriptive. Far closer to the truth would be "teacher-student," with all the clear priorities of self-concern that ordering contains. Then there is the code phrase "us *and* them," more respectable than "student-teacher" because more truthful in its description. "And" has a fine ambiguity in our language—as in mother *and* child, black *and* white—which allows equally substitution of *against* and *for* in the phrase "us *and* them." I propose substitution of *for* in the code phrase, a replacement which not only reorders priorities but which also redefines the nature of ethical actions.

Meaningful substitution of *for* in the descriptive relationship of teachers to students would succeed in expanding the number of possible responses to questions of "What can *I* do?" and "What *more* can I do?" by permitting the previously indefensible viewpoint that the system is less important than the child, individually or collectively, and that self-protection is less important than child-protection in the hierarchy of pedagogical values. Restructuring the code in this way leads to significant change in notions of ethical action: For example, I believe it makes a league with children one probable and ethical choice available to teachers; I also believe that it places a double burden of judgment and risk upon those who accept its mandate.

This double burden is equally composed of judging what is best for children and what is tolerable for self. Neither decision is easy, but both offer themselves for resolution by the individual teacher in ways impossible under the current code. Heretofore, what is best for children has been regarded as inseparable from the question of what is best for the system. No other explanation fully accounts for the revulsion which conspiracy with children against the system (and against individuals who compose it) inspires in so many. Conspiring with children is simply not playing the game. Because it is not, and the game demands playing, its rules must be revised.

Revision of the rules not only raises the ethical problem of manipulating children—not a new problem, but one with new dimensions if the child is to be regarded as more important than the institution—but also raises the intensely personal problem of justifiable risk. In introducing this discussion I spoke of the "most serious internal problem in American public education." I believe it is this: That teachers are so uncertain of their professional identity and mission that they risk nothing of themselves either in fulfilling that identity or in accomplishing that mission. In short, they seldom if ever can be brought to the point where they would sooner lose their jobs than their identity. Since one is a palpable loss while the other is not, teachers have learned to be content with survival. Even at the cost of themselves, even at the cost of children's hope and education.

20

I CAME LATE to that March meeting with the full school faculty. I don't recall what delayed me, but I do remember that the interior shape of the meeting room was changed. For the first time in more than half a year, chairs were not spread through the room in ranks whose density increased in proportion to their distance from the front. Miraculously, the room had no glowering depth, for seats were arranged in a large crescent around a chair reserved for me. Though the significance of the new arrangement struck me as I entered the room, I did not immediately realize the full meaning of signs and symbols of change displayed during that memorable afternoon.

If the first sign of change was the arrangement of chairs, the second was the distribution of their occupants. Until I saw them together as a group, I did not realize how much the mood and commitment of the faculty had changed during the first month of the new semester. The difference between one-third disposed and one-third indisposed may sound more rhetorical than real, but it is a profound difference when viewed in terms of bodies instead of words. In place of the thin, hard line of supporters at the front of the room that I was accustomed to beholding, I now beheld a thin, hard line of antagonists at the rear of the room. Thin lines, however hard, do not glower with much effect.

A gentle sense of jubilance pervaded the room, almost as though we were discreetly celebrating victory with concern for the present vanquished. Our usual practice was to begin with a report summarizing some aspect of the intervening period, and then to base our discussion upon what we had heard. Our reporter for this meeting was the librarian, a competent woman who supervised her pitiful collection from the confines of a room with floor space appropriate to the books. Though she bore up bravely beneath the burden of books that no child in his right mind would touch, much less remove from the shelf and read, she was beginning to show some strain at the end of the first semester. No one can withstand the destructive experience of continued failure; she knew as well as the children that her books were not for reading.

Her report transfigured her face and transformed the mood of the meeting. Gentle jubilance became outspoken joy as the librarian recited statistics of usage which would have convinced a jury of her peers that she was far too inventive to be reliable. Perhaps the most interesting aspect of her reception by the group is that no one questioned her veracity. There are countless respectable ways of calling a fellow faculty member a liar, but not a single one of the fifty-odd people in that room challenged her remarkable figures. Which means, I think, that everyone in that room believed such a difference could be made in the reading habits of children.

I call attention to that belief because I have discovered its existence in teachers and schools where every piece of evidence weighs against its presence. How to explain teach-

ers' and administrators' equanimity in the face of evidence
that children who would read nothing suddenly seem to be
reading everything? Most probable seems to me to be the
explanation that a great many teachers—especially teachers
of unpromising students—have given up personal hope of
improving the world they teach in. Their belief in what is
possible does not shrink; what does atrophy, however, is
their belief in what is possible for them. Having lost hope
themselves, they communicate hopelessness to their students
who soon learn to regard their education with full measure
of despair.

Though they are not prepared to believe in themselves
as agents of change, these same defeated teachers are quite
willing to accept that role in others. It is just this passive
acceptance which accounts for short-term success and long-
term failure of so much that is begun but never completed
in the schools.

A customary procedure, for example, is to have someone
inside or outside the school perceive an unfulfilled need and
then resolve to change the school to meet the need. Though
much depends upon the quality of his determination, a reso-
lute agent usually discovers that change is not difficult to
make. At the point of innovation, faculty passivity is more
nearly an asset than a liability. Those who do not assist,
generally do not care enough to impede. Having long been
accustomed to a spectator's role, they are unlikely to abandon it either for help or hindrance. "After all," begins their
credo, "what can one person do?" The answer they offer
and expect is "Nothing."

Unfortunately, however, their habitual response is insufficient to guarantee vital continuance of change in the schools.
No single teacher and very few small groups of teachers—
much less administrators or visiting experts—can effect
more than brief and ephemeral alterations in public education. Passivity may permit entrance but it will not supply

nurture. The largely passive faculties of schools for the impoverished are powerful guarantees against hope for the children who inhabit them.

The librarian spoke and I exulted. Questions were asked, discussions begun, stories shared, and I had all I could do to keep from pounding the desk and roaring for joy. Could a grown man, fifteen years a teacher, take so great a pleasure from so small a fact as increased library usage? He could; he did. Children were pouring into that inadequate little room carved out of the school's most remote corner, and books were pouring out. Children awaited its opening in the morning and bemoaned its closing in the afternoon; it had become a room for children instead of a closet for ghosts.

As I write this and recall the sweetness of that afternoon, I cannot help but juxtapose against that memory a child's response to a question asked by the staff of the University of Colorado's Hospital School in Denver. The fact that the School treats *disturbing* rather than *disturbed* children reveals its belief that the illness lies in a disturbed society which too often transfers its affliction to children, preferring to analyze and sequester them rather than to examine itself. One of these disturbing children was asked on a written test to complete a sentence that began, "I would rather read than ———." The word the child supplied was "die."

What we heard reported that afternoon was the existence of many children who would rather read than not read, and a surprising number who would rather read than do anything else. That such preferences should seem extraordinary enough to mention, is testimony to the depth of our failure and the breadth of our success. As teachers we have failed to convince children of what we ourselves do not believe—that reading is for pleasure or that extensive reading is necessary—and we have succeeded in perpetuating the unhappiest tradition of our own educations.

The tradition I refer to is the mythical child of the truth

that "I became an English teacher because I always liked to read." So long as the statement is understood to obtain its validity from the perfect past, it remains believable. Once it is viewed as having something to do with the present, then truth requires a single alteration: *Always* liked to read becomes *once* liked to read, and the statement retains its credibility. It also helps to explain the creation of antiliterate legions in schools all over the country.

Having once liked to read and having become reasonably proficient at it, children who are admired by adults because they like to read become adolescents who are admired because they read well. Pleasure is replaced by performance, which has its own pleasures; the adolescent becomes the young adult whose college degree suddenly removes his reason for performing. Having become a teacher and having long ago sold his birthright of pleasure for the pottage of performance, he can only teach what he knows: how to read, not how to like to read. And so he re-creates himself where he can, and where he cannot he views his students as unpromising.

More than that, he resists new materials because new materials must be read and he does not like to read. He becomes, finally, the teacher revealed in a research project reported to the United States Office of Education:

It was often evident that many teachers knew very little about what books were appropriate for specific grade levels. Although a sufficient number of books were available for these grades, the teachers did not know they existed. They lacked familiarity with paperbound editions, and, more important, with the library resources which provide such information. It was found, too, that many were uninformed about recent professional publications and research data. An even more depressing revelation was the discovery that many teachers themselves were nonreaders and seldom read beyond the texts used by their students. How can such classroom teachers generate an interest in reading? How will these teachers create the lifetime reading habit accepted as a goal in the elementary and high school reading program?

The questions are rhetorical, the answers painfully apparent. Perhaps as rare as habitual kindness, the "lifetime reading habit" is no more the province of teachers than students. But as I listened to the librarian's beautiful statistics, I could bring myself to believe that such a habit could grow upon the children whose happiness she was describing.

One sign more awaited me in that afternoon's meeting, but the sign is difficult to describe. More than two years later, in a factory town near Birmingham in the English Midlands, I had a similar experience. Beginning there is easier, perhaps because the second experience was with a child.

I had come to visit this Midlands school in July, on the last day before the children were to begin their long vacation. All work was done for the year, but the teacher was kind enough to teach a brief English lesson to her immigrant Indian and Pakistani children, using materials in which I had special interest. When she was done we talked and then I was free to wander amongst the students who were themselves free to do as they liked within the room. A group was playing a form of rummy which I watched with interest. When the hand was finished, one of them asked me if I could do a card trick and then passed me the deck when I admitted that I could.

"Name any number between one and thirteen," I said as I shuffled the cards. My intention was to manipulate the number to the point where it described a card whose location I already knew.

"Two of spades," said the boy who had given me the cards.

"Turn over the top card," I said. He did. It was the two of spades. Shock waves passed through their hands and faces like wind through wheat. Then the boy who had supplied number and suit when I had asked only for number, and who had with magnificent improbability named one of the two cards (top and bottom) whose location I knew in the deck, leaned toward me, put his hand on mine, and said something in his native tongue.

I do not know to this day what he said, but I do know it doesn't matter. The words were less than the light, dry touch of his hand which told me that a special thing had happened and he was thanking me for it. In some parts of the American South this is called "hands-on." It is a way of talking to people whom you like, a way of talking with or without words, an ancient language that overgoes boundaries and tongues.

That ancient language was spoken to me on a Thursday afternoon in March in a large room on the second floor of a junior high school in northwest Washington, D.C. In more than six months only the children, the principal, and a single teacher had spoken to me in that tongue. Within the space of an hour, a dozen and more of the faculty touched my arm, my hand, my shoulder—reaching out from their seats, speaking with me at the front of the room, stopping me afterwards in the hall—and those who spoke to me in that way were of both sexes and various colors.

What they said with their hands we both tried to say with words: We had come through, and we were immensely grateful for each other's help. No prognosis for the future was asked or offered. It was enough to have that hour of success. We all knew well enough that things fall apart, and the knowledge made us more grateful for a moment's hope and coherence.

21

THE SPRING EQUINOX marked not only a change of season inside and outside the school, it also marked a change in composition of the gang. Cicero was the name of the change, and I was indirectly responsible for his adoption by the group.

Cicero was a child of poverty by any standard other than the name he bore. Called "Sis" by all who knew him (except his teachers who did not know him or did not care to know him and therefore persisted in addressing him by the full name of Cicero which he hated for its queer difference from the names of all his friends), he was distinguished for his sudden violence even amongst violent children. Few of his peers and fewer of his teachers could understand what he said, though any sign of incomprehension usually drove him to rage. Since he always mumbled, mispronounced, looked away from his listeners, and spoke in a monotone, he was often misunderstood and frequently enraged.

Sis and I met in his uncle's poolroom. We met when he walked up to me, moving as nearly sideways as a human being can, examined the remains of the game I had just finished, and asked (without ever looking toward me at all): "Wahshoopoo?" Snapper, who was standing by my side and with whom I had just played, answered for me: "Man, he eat you up. You don't wanna mess none with him." Had Snapper not responded so that I could deduce the question from the answer, I might never have known I had been invited to shoot a game of pool.

Sis and I became poolroom acquaintances. Whenever I came in, always in the company of Cleo's gang, no matter what the time of day, he was there, walking and looking sideways, caught between the desire to shoot pool and the desire for effacement, suffering a paroxysm of abnegation and self-denial. By noticing no one, he hoped not to be noticed. Perhaps his constant attendance in the cool, semi-dark poolroom with only the tables caught in the circles of light, was part of the same attempt. He was fully present only when he shot pool or fell into a sudden rage.

Sis's chief and perhaps only accomplishment when I met him was his pool game. For a man it would have been admirable; for a fourteen-year-old boy it was magnificent. Even Snapper, who was our resident expert, deferred to Sis's considerable skill. Because enforced deference did nothing to improve Snapper's disposition, the joy in his voice was undisguised when he told Sis to keep out of my way.

That first meeting in the poolroom is the apparent beginning of Sis's story, but it takes its true origins from all the years Sis and I spent in various poolrooms before we met each other. Though he was only fourteen, he had literally grown up in poolrooms since his uncle and guardian had owned or managed one during all his nephew's life. But his uncle was more than an owner or manager; he was a good second-class pool hustler, and he had taught Sis his craft.

For those unfamiliar with the trade, let me explain that

the term "second-class pool hustler" has no opprobrium attached. Any hustler worthy of the name knows that the country boasts a few first-class hustlers, perhaps no more than several dozen, and that all the rest of the profession is second-class or less. Since the lesser tend to be the non-survivors, local pool sharks who still have their bankrolls can usually claim a place amongst the estimable second-class.

Though I had no uncle or guardian to train me, I devoted more hours to shooting pool between the ages of twelve and twenty-two than I spent on any other activity except sleeping. At eighteen, after graduation from high school, I hitch-hiked to Miami Beach with the intention of trying my hand at the mecca of the profession. When I withdrew my hand after several months of trying, it was empty and I had learned a lesson in definition: They were first-class, I was second-class, and I had better do what best fitted my abilities as a second-class hustler; I went to college.

I have recounted this piece of history because it was directly responsible for my contact with Sis. In a conversation with the gang I once said that I understood how Althea Gibson felt when she entitled her autobiography *I Always Wanted To Be Somebody*. I was prompted to the comment because Wentworth had asked me if I was what I wanted to be, and my eye had fallen on the book Cleo was carrying and reading for the third time.

"I don't know," I said. "All I ever really wanted to be was a first-class pool hustler and I wasn't good enough. Outside of that, I guess I felt like Althea Gibson. I wanted to be somebody important."

"You shoot pool?" Snapper was surprised and interested.

"Not much any more. But I used to play a lot."

"Got you own stick?"

"Yes."

"I got my own too."

It was my turn to be surprised. Not many thirteen-year-old boys, especially poor ones, have their own sticks.

"Two piece?"

"Sure. Sis's uncle give it to me."

"Who?"

"Dumbhead in the seventh grade. His uncle own a poolroom." Uncle Wiggly volunteered the information.

"He ain't no dumbhead."

"He fourteen in the seventh grade. Ain't no smarthead."

"What you know?" Snapper was angry but Uncle Wiggly wasn't backing down. Then, to me: "Sis work a lot for his uncle. Rack man. Clean up. All kinda thing. Don't get to come to school much. But he ain't no dumbhead. And he shoot *some* stick."

Our conversation went from Sis to his uncle's poolroom to the fact that it wasn't so far away, especially with a car, to Snapper's desire to see me handle a cue. Could we go in my car and shoot a couple of games? Even Cleo was interested. I was the only one who didn't want to go, and I told them why:

"Being a white man here at school is different from being a white man in a black man's poolroom."

"Couple white men come in ever' day from the stores on the Avenue. Don't shoot good, but they white."

They talked it out. Wentworth made the decision because Cleo had only once been in a poolroom. He pointed out that two white men from the stores at lunchtime might be different from a white stranger in the late afternoon. Since Snapper would play with me, Snapper should find out if we could all go into Sis's poolroom.

"How much your cue weigh?"

"Nineteen ounces."

"He really know." I had passed Snapper's test. He would undertake Wentworth's commission.

I had expected to meet Sis when I went to his uncle's poolroom but Snapper, after examining the faces, said that he was nowhere in sight. Then I forgot about him as I met his uncle who gave me one of his own jointed cues to play with and set us up on the best table in the house. In fact I forgot everything but the balls as I played to my gallery of five companions and to another, larger gallery of discreetly watching eyes. After half a dozen games with Snapper, who was a good pool shot and a better loser, Sis appeared and made the invitation that Snapper translated in response.

"I tough meat." Sis, still looking at no one, in answer to Snapper's warning.

"He got long teeth," Snapper replied, obviously enjoying himself.

"Break 'em off on my hide."

Listening carefully, it was possible to understand what Sis was saying. He sounded unpracticed. A strange thing to think of a fourteen-year-old boy in the midst of a big city, but speech sounded like an alien activity for him. What was most wrong were his rhythms and emphases. "Break 'em off on my hide" was actually very close to "Bre koff'n mide." I tried to induce him to talk with me as we played.

"You shoot a good stick."

"Youshoo bear."

"Been at it twenty-five years."

"So'ee," with a movement of his head toward a man playing on a nearby table.

"He could play another twenty-five and it wouldn't make any difference. Couple more years for you, you'll be able to wipe me out." To which he replied something that escaped me completely. While he was shooting, I looked quizically at Snapper who hesitated before answering—"He say 'brown pertaters.'"

"Brown potatoes?" I said, not sure I had heard him correctly. "What does that mean?"

"Horseshit," said Snapper in a choked whisper.

I turned to the table in time to see Sis miss a relatively easy shot and leave the cue ball in a difficult position. "It all yours," he said. "Easy pickin's."

"Easy pickings?" I said as I searched for a shot. "Brown potatoes." I watched his face out of the corner of my eye. He scowled, and I thought I had lost him. I remembered that first interview with Wentworth and Cleo . . . had I misapplied the lesson? Then the scowl relaxed and he said clearly. "Reckon' it ain't the best leave in the worl'."

In the car on the way back to Tenth Street Snapper said it for all of us: "I holdin' my breath when you say *brown pertaters* to Sis. He an awful touchy cat."

"Yes," I said, "I was watching his face."

"Me, too." Wentworth, quietly. "Gonna jump him did he twitch."

"He a creep," put in Uncle Wiggly. "I glad you whip his ass."

"He ain't no creep." It was Cleo with the first words she'd said all afternoon. "He just a scared rabbit."

"Huh! What *he* scared of?"

"Ever'thing."

"Yeah," said Wentworth, reflectively, "he even scared of hisself."

For the next three months, until early June, we shot pool weekly at Sis's poolroom. It became a ritual for me to begin with Snapper and progress to Sis. The more we played together, the more I recognized the justice of Cleo's and Wentworth's remarks. Sis seemed a child without a skin, an ambulant collection of nerve endings that shrieked at the slightest contact. As he became more accustomed to me, he became somewhat easier. But the real change in him had little to do with me and everything to do with Cleo and Wentworth, who performed as generous an act of personal charity as I have ever known.

Though Sis was not a boy you'd notice in a crowd, he was tall enough to be painfully visible amongst his classmates in the seventh grade. The physical difference in height between twelve- and thirteen-year olds, and a fourteen-year old who shuffles with his head down, is not as great as it might be, but it is still enough to draw the eye. I found myself noticing Sis in the school's corridors as I had never noticed him before. Was it solely because I had not known him? Considering his comparative size and peculiar gait, that seemed an unlikely explanation. Why was he suddenly so apparent? I stumbled upon the explanation when I arrived at school earlier than usual on a Friday morning.

As I parked in front of school a hand opened my curbside door and a familiar voice said, "Sis say he gon' tear you up this afternoon."

I slid across the seat from behind the wheel in time to hear another familiar voice say, "Aw, naw, man, don' say that. Catch enough trouble from him without he get all het up." Sis and Cleo were standing behind Wentworth on the sidewalk. The four of us walked into school together, where Wentworth and Sis left us to do some business in the gym before classes began.

"Cleo," I said, remembering the situation reversed in the previous autumn, "how come you're messing on Sis?"

"That ain't . . . ," she started to deny before she realized what I had said. She grinned, then confirmed what I began to understand when I saw the three of them together on the sidewalk. For the past month she and Wentworth had been collecting Sis every morning on their way to school. What he wouldn't tolerate from the other three, even Snapper who was his friend, he'd allow to Wentworth and herself. She thought it might be because they were older and he knew Wentworth could do him if he had to, or just because he wanted somebody to look in on him.

Whatever the reason, he was now making it to school

every day in their company and he seemed to like the arrangement. His problem had always been that his uncle went to bed late and got up late and nobody woke Sis up for school. Cleo reflected for a moment on Sis's situation, then said something I'll never forget. I wonder how many adults in her life it described: "It ain't that his uncle a bad man," she said, trying to explain what had happened to Sis. "It just that he ain't good enough."

Not long after I found the answer to Sis's sudden visibility in the school corridors, Cleo came to me with a more serious problem. Sis's homeroom teacher had as much as said he couldn't hope to be put up to the eighth grade no matter how much he came to school now, because his attendance had been so bad during the first semester.

"He don' get permoted," she told me, "nobody see him 'round here no more. You talk to that teacher. She listen to you."

What, I wanted to know, could I say? I too wouldn't be around next year because my work would be done. She and Wentworth would be going up the hill to the high school. Who would look after Sis? Who would keep him coming to school?

"Me an' Wentworth done already talked 'bout that," she told me. "Iff'n Sis won't 'low Snapper and Rubbergut to come for him, we gon' keep right on wakin' him an' fetchin' him." The mild disbelief I felt must have reflected itself in my face, because then she told me that they were doing a lot more than waking Sis in the morning. Sis was a drinker because his uncle was a drinker who didn't mind if Sis had one every now and then for himself. Trouble was, since nobody was around to feed him, Sis found it easier to drink than eat. Maybe he didn't like it so much, but a couple beers or a little lightning and he wasn't hungry enough to bother with eating.

Wentworth and she had been fixing breakfast for him every morning while he got himself together. Sometimes the two of them ate first, sometimes they brought food and ate with him. Either way, he got something to eat to start the day so he didn't have to drink until later. Nothing they could do about what happened in the poolroom, but something to eat in the morning and hot food for lunch at school could make a difference.

She looked me full in the eyes, then, perhaps wondering if she had said enough to guarantee my intervention. Whatever she saw there must not have satisfied her because she went on to give me one last piece of information:

"We teachin' him," she said, almost inaudibly.

"What?" I asked, meaning only to have her repeat what she had said.

"We teachin' him to talk better."

They were, and the results were in school and poolroom for all to hear. Dramatic changes usually reserve themselves for stage or screen. Sis's change was truer to the pace of real life—it was slow, for his tutors (and for him) it must have been painfully slow, but it was perceptible. By the first week in June he had become a boy who spoke better than anyone had a right to expect in March. In his case, better meant clearer, sometimes so much clearer that he did not sound like the same boy who had once asked me "wahshoopoo?"

Both Cleo and Wentworth talked to me about the methods they were using. The first approach was, for them, the most natural one: Since paperbound books were all over school, and both children were constantly carrying a book with them—Wentworth had begun to read openly in his English class, though if pressed by the teacher he would deny comprehension—they had begun by reading to Sis and having him read to them. It was Wentworth, discovering that Sis could read aloud better than he could talk aloud, who made an imaginative leap into the absent dimension of Sis's life that so deeply affected his speech:

As Wentworth put it, "His problem be he ain't got nobody to talk to. *Never* had nobody to talk to." When I had thought that Sis sounded unpracticed in his speech, I was groping for the answer that Wentworth found. Sis lived in a one-child world, where conversation with anyone was a rarity. Though his singularity was unusual, his need to use and to hear his own voice was not. In that, he was no different from the rest of us; unlike our school experience, however, his was drawn from the well of silence into which unpromising children are dropped as soon as possible.

Cleo and Wentworth fed and read to him, the whole group talked to him, and I went to speak with his teacher about next year. Had it been necessary I would have gone to the principal, because Sis was becoming a fair risk for the future. The attention he was getting had made him think better of himself. Though change in his speech was the children's first aim, they were actually making more rapid gains with his appearance and his carriage.

Sis always looked thrown together, as though he had met his clothes by accident in a windstorm. His clothes, his shuffle, and his sliding eyes combined to make him look absent. No other word seems to describe the odd impression he gave of being about to disappear. It was just that impression which was most radically altered by the children's attention. As spring drew toward summer, Sis sometimes looked and sounded as though he had opted for the world.

His homeroom teacher laid bare for me another aspect of the interior lives of children like Sis who speak the language of failure. When I asked her about Sis's chances of promotion for the following year, she was mildly surprised.

Cicero hadn't missed a day for so long, had been so different from the peculiar boy she was familiar with, that she saw no reason to question his June promotion. Had I special reason for asking?

I repeated to her what Cleo had told me. The teacher shook her head, an expression of resigned despair on her face, and told me what she had said. She was reasonably certain of her words, as she might not have been with another child, because she had been so pleased by the change in Cicero's attendance and appearance. What she had said was gratulatory: If Cicero had continued his attendance of the first semester, he could not have hoped for promotion. But the change in him during the second semester was certainly remarkable, and she hoped he would be able to keep it up.

She was, on reflection, not entirely surprised that he had misunderstood her. Though he was a strange specimen, she was too well acquainted with children like him to think that they always understood what she said. Especially when good and bad were mixed into the same comment; too often, they would hear only the bad. It was almost as if they *wanted* to hear bad things about themselves. She knew that was a peculiar thing to say, but in her experience it seemed to be true.

She was anxious to talk about children like Cicero, because she found their number growing while her ability to help them appeared to be decreasing. What seemed to her to characterize them was an expectation and acceptance of failure so profound that they were actually suspicious of praise and almost indifferent to criticism. Cicero might be exceptional in the variety of his problems, but he was certainly not unique in kind. She knew another dozen boys and girls in his class alone who would be as likely to misunderstand her comment. Not *willfully* misunderstand, mind you, but more like *habitually* misunderstand. It was almost as though they had no place in their lives for success.

And there was another odd thing about them that had confused her during this past year. They were the ones, these children like Cicero, who were the greatest enemies to change in the school. Just the ones you'd think would be happiest to see old texts replaced by newspapers, magazines, and paperbound books—they were the ones who complained most about the change. But then they were the ones who complained about all change, who held so desperately to anything that was familiar no matter how much pain and anguish it had given them.

Her description of these children led me to tell her about an experience with similar children in the Maxey Boys Training School. The occasion was the boys' first English class, a time when they were given paperbound dictionaries and other softbound materials which were to be their English textbooks. The reaction of a significant minority is summed in the response of one: "Shoot, *these* ain't no textbooks. How we gonna learn anything with books like these?"

Many of them were disappointed and said so. Their disappointment and unhappiness was in proportion to their failure: The worse their previous school experience, the more vociferous and prolonged their complaint. We were unprepared for their reaction and frankly amazed. No one had told us—had no one known enough to tell us?—that there is a species of child so wounded in his pride and self-esteem that he cannot be comfortable with symbols of potential change. Give him the old symbols, however miserable the experience they represent, for with them at least he can estimate his pain. Pain foreknown may be bearable; the unknown anguish of new experience may topple even the sturdiest sufferer.

Contrary to a widely held and comforting belief, such

children are not primarily the clientele of penal schools and they are not a minor species of insignificant number. They are found throughout the public schools at all levels of privilege and income, and they are far too numerous to be treated with the luxury of ignorance. The child who learns to disregard himself becomes the adult who values himself little and others less. The self-destruction of failure courted and won in the schools can too easily become the other-destruction of rancor and bitterness spilled in the streets.

22

COMMUNITY AND STUDENTS are the two resources least used by public education from kindergarten through junior college. Since the community is not composed of qualified educators, it cannot be called upon for more than money and nominal supervision. Since students are learners, they cannot be teachers. Both arguments are as specious as they are obvious, but their speciousness seems to be clearer at a distance than it is nearby. My purpose here, however, is not to argue for the expanded use of nonprofessional adults within the schools; rather, it is to argue for using students to teach students at every level and opportunity. I do not argue for the first because I believe it to be inevitable. The second, though more important, seems to me less likely of realization.

Failure to use students as teachers of students is made more remarkable by the nature of an experience shared by all teachers. No one who has taught has been able to avoid the humbling, edifying experience of learning through teaching. Most teachers of English to whom I have spoken have agreed that they understood little of English grammar and rhetoric until they attempted to teach the structure and force of the language to their students. To that point, they regarded themselves as teachers. At that point, they became students and found themselves understanding by analysis what before they had learned by rote.

How can so universal a learning experience fail of application to one of teaching's most pervasive problems? What are pleas for smaller classes about if not about attention to children who need it most and receive it least? No teacher can pay sufficient attention to the learning needs of twenty-five children, much less the customary thirty-five and more. But classes may be halved when budgets are doubled; doubled budgets and the millenium will arrive together. Until they do, teachers will have classes that are impossibly large so long as they do not enlist the aid of their students as teachers. When they solicit that aid, they may discover that neither the millenium nor a doubled budget is necessary.

Cleo and Wentworth were making daily discoveries about the double responsibility of teaching. For example, Cleo had always looked well. Though a plain child with an angular face, she combined the life of her eyes with the style of her dress into an attractive whole. Shaping Sis into something that looked more planned than accidental was a natural function of her own control and coherence. Not so, however, with Wentworth, for the attention he gave Sis reflected itself sooner in teacher than pupil. The change in Wentworth was as apparent as it was instructive.

Measured against the benchmark of his dress and demeanor on the occasion of our visit to the University of Maryland, Wentworth was a truculent ragbag. Knowing him as friend and colleague rather than adversary and student had led me to understand that both truculence and disarray were designed to ward off schoolhouse dragons.

From some point in the past of conscious decision until the equally conscious alternatives of the ninth grade, Wentworth's disguise had been exceptionally effective. Though his dress and public manner were altered by his earlier decision to "do it different," the change was insufficient to guard him against the onslaught of self-consciousness that accompanied his new relationship with Sis.

If the change in Sis was noticeable, in Wentworth it was unmistakable. Just as few students understand a subject until they are forced to the analysis and explanation of teaching, so do few Wentworths understand themselves until they view their reflections in another child's eyes. Wentworth had been breaking through the shell of his self-created environment before he and Cleo took on the project of Sis's survival. In the last three months of the school year, breaking turned into shattering as he saw himself through Sis's eyes and determined to admire what he saw.

Though the most apparent change in Wentworth was in his dress and his demeanor—daily he became more like the confident, stylish leader who had handled our problems at the University of Maryland—a less obvious and parallel change was taking place in his public speech. In this he was joined by Cleo who more frequently allowed herself to venture beyond the protective thicket of black argot. Both of them had been surprised into further awareness and vulnerability by a two-edged sword they employed to cut some of the incoherence from Sis's speech. The weapon they were using was a tape recorder.

When I discovered the tutorial relationship between my friends and Sis, and considered Wentworth's insight into the genesis of Sis's problem, I thought of a potential remedy I had been anxious to use with similar children in a classroom situation. Because the year had been so difficult, I had not been able to initiate classroom experiments in language using a tape recorder as alter ego for children with impoverished speech. Here, unexpectedly, was my chance, even if the classroom was a kitchen table in the two-room apartment Sis shared with his uncle.

The idea of tape recorder as language remedy had come from the success of some social studies teachers in expanding children's identity and awareness with the device of role playing: Do you think so little of yourself that you cannot play yourself to any effect? Then play somebody else— anybody else—and give yourself opportunity to expand. In gentle hands the device can be extraordinarily successful, for it allows the child with impoverished ego to feed himself on fictitious identities. Belle Kaufman's story in *Up The Down Staircase* of the boy who signed himself "Me" in a sigh of self-effacement illustrates role playing at its best. Though disregard of self was his habit, he could and did play the role of judge in a mock court with competence and grace. More important, his success in that alternate identity caused positive change in his view of himself.

If projection of person, then why not projection of language? Role playing in its full realization implies both being someone else and seeing yourself through other eyes. The player assumes the attributes of another personality not only because he briefly becomes that other person, but also because in his new role he is able to view himself as he was and to choose in part to be another. It is this second function of role playing that led me to provide Cleo and Wentworth with a tape recorder for their work with Sis.

Perhaps the primary thrust of language education is the effort to have the student hear himself. So long as child or adult is blocked from the sound of himself—whether by himself or by the instructor; whether in his written or his spoken language—attempted remediation of his language problems is hopeless. Apparent change may easily be obtained, but it is certain to be ephemeral in its effect for it will be based upon supervision rather than comprehension. The privileged child who does not hear himself may become the adult who offends the ears of his society. The impoverished child who does not hear himself relinquishes one powerful weapon in his battle for survival.

Sis's first reaction to hearing himself, as reported by his tutors, was a classic one: "Ain't me," he said, when Wentworth played his first tape back to him.

"Know how he feel," added Wentworth. "When I heard me, didn't want it to *be* me."

Sis obviously felt the same way, only he felt it in proportion to the greater pain of hearing his own mumbled and garbled speech. Cleo and Wentworth had taped him surreptitiously one morning at breakfast after nullifying the instrument's presence by using it to record and replay music from Sis's transistor radio. Pretending to switch the machine off, Wentworth changed it instead to "record" and preserved Sis's morning discourse. They reported considerable difficulty in convincing Sis that it was really his voice on that tape.

Conversation, reading aloud and being read to, using the tape recorder—Sis joined the rest of the blossoming things that spring season. And his tutors joined him. While Cleo and Wentworth spoke with admiration and even amazement of the change in Sis, they did not see him through unprejudiced eyes. Their pride in his speech, his appearance, and his school attendance was also an understandable if unexpressed pride in themselves for what they had achieved. Had they been able to see themselves, they would have had even more reason for their delight.

Both Cleo and Wentworth were reaping the rich harvest of their roles as teachers. Listening to Sis speak and read, they listened to themselves as well. Not liking what they heard, their interior ear attuned to a new sense of fit and form, they each attempted to satisfy their individual notions of appropriate language. Cleo's decision about her speech, as conscious as Wentworth's about his life style, was equally effective. Often when speaking to me alone, sometimes with Wentworth present, occasionally before the full gang —she spoke an English as clear and error-free as any bright ninth-grade child of any color.

I have added the last phrase purposefully. Just as I refused to accept Rob's judgment of my proper relationship to the five children, so also I deny the notion that black lower-class children should not be required to learn standard English. More than that, I am willing publicly to defend the practice of teaching standard English to all children even when it is attacked on the grounds that to teach standard English is to teach middle-class values. I also believe that those who would deny the relationship between teaching the language and inculcating the values of a language community are no less dangerous than those who would forbid the black child access to the language of the dominant class.

The truth is, I believe, that we inevitably teach who we are and what we value even as we teach how we write and how we speak. To deny these simultaneous actions is to deny our existence. No language has meaning apart from objects and concepts it represents, and no one who has spent five minutes with introductory reading texts would deny that even the simplest representation of objects and concepts reflects from all surfaces the values and judgments of its maker. Of course we propagandize for our way of life as we teach the language which represents it. Though we can do no less, we are not absolved from the obligation of restraint even as we proselytize.

Restraint is a condition of mind reflected in control of action. In the specific action of teaching standard English to impoverished children who speak a dialect, the required restraint can be the product of a simple sense of fair play (sometimes known as human decency, not always recognized as a necessary component in relationships between adults and children) or it can be produced by an equally simple concern for the child's survival. No matter which cause, the effect will be the same: No child will be required to lose himself while assuming other identities.

These noble intentions, usually spoken of in terms of "respecting the child's integrity," are too often translated into teaching several modern black classics while extolling the accomplishments of George Washington Carver and Jackie Robinson. What is wanted instead is admiration—admiration for the independent self which children construct from disparate fragments, admiration for the structural strength of patchwork identities which refuse to fracture and explode beneath the pressure of constant attack.

We who so easily find a place in our society for both the creations and aberrations of producing artists, must not deny equal freedoms to impoverished children. Like the creative maker in society, they too perceive an uncommon world, and *they too live in the world they perceive*. When the nature of their chief accomplishment—survival—is fully appreciated, they too may best be understood as producing artists, giving coherence to fragments, creating a momentary beauty where none existed before.

23

SIS CAME TO SCHOOL one Thursday morning in May wearing his shades. Which would have been entirely unremarkable had he removed them soon after entering the building, because he always wore sunglasses on bright days. A poolshooter's eyes are his one indispensable asset; since poolrooms are usually underlit by lamplight and unviolated by natural light, hustlers of all ages and qualifications often wear dark glasses during their ventures into the sun. Though fourteen is early to develop such sensitivity, Sis at that age had spent ten years in his uncle's poolrooms.

On this Thursday morning Sis had his shades on when Cleo and Wentworth went to his apartment for breakfast and he still wore them when he sat in his first class of the day. Both Cleo and Wentworth had thought the dark glasses a little strong for breakfast, but only Wentworth had experience enough to suspect the reason for their presence:

"When I seen them," he told us at the end of the day, "I knowed he was hidin' his eyes. Figured he been hit by lightnin'."

Anyone who has been "hit by lightning" has been on a drinking binge with hard liquor. So far as Wentworth's intuition went, it was right. Sis had been drinking with his uncle early that morning and the dark glasses hid his ravaged eyes. But he was wearing glasses less to hide the fact that he had been hit by lightning than that he had also been hit by his uncle. His left eye was swollen shut and surrounded by bruised, split flesh. Had his first-period teacher not made the terrible mistake of snatching the glasses from his eyes, Wentworth would have kept his suspicions to himself and Sis would have been spared the agony of revelation.

My first intimation of disaster came when I entered the cafeteria and almost stepped on Uncle Wiggly: "Cleo want to know could you set with us?" he said as I loomed over him. I knew that only an emergency could force Cleo to speak with me in the cafeteria. She had always been careful to make no claims within the school upon our friendship, and her boys had followed her lead. The conference to which I was being invited could have no happy cause.

It had none, but the full depth of its unhappiness was hidden from all but one of us until we met at 4:30 that afternoon on the school steps. Wentworth was missing from the conference in the cafeteria because he had been sent by Cleo to find and comfort Sis. Find him he did, at the kitchen table in his uncle's apartment, again caught in a storm and struck by lightning, almost incoherent with alcohol and rage. But we did not know any of this until after school.

I had never sat with the group before; as I followed Uncle Wiggly to their table, I realized that various children and adults were interested in my destination. But I had little time to think of them, for I had barely reached the table and noted Wentworth's absence before Cleo greeted me with her characteristic lack of amenities: "Sis in bad trouble."

"What did he do?" As I said it I realized that I could have asked "What happened to him?" Just beneath the surface I am an instinctive accusor of children.

"Wore his shades to school and wouldn't take 'em off."

I don't know what dress rules were in effect for girls at Garnet-Patterson, but boys had only to conform to two that went beyond common decency: no dark glasses and no hats worn inside the building. Insist on wearing either in the classroom and you were certain to be sent to the principal's office; persist in keeping your cover and you were likely to be sent home. The crime was fairly common. Sis must have given it a special twist.

"What happened?"

"Teacher grab 'em, he grab 'em back. Teacher say he hit her."

"What does he say?"

"Nothin'. He gone." He gone. A return under pressure to the black argot, and yet she was speaking to me. A foot in both worlds, precarious but necessary.

"He didn't hit her none." Snapper, unable to contain himself any longer. In several months of seeing Sis with Cleo and Wentworth, I had forgotten that Snapper was Sis's original friend and partisan. Now his agitated face and voice reflected that relationship.

Between Cleo and Snapper I got all the information the gang had to give. After the first period of the day, one of Sis's classmates had told Snapper about Sis's trouble. Snapper found Wentworth who took the story to Cleo. After they had confirmed the details by questioning other members of Sis's class, Wentworth went to look for Sis during lunch period.

Half a dozen members of Sis's class had seen the incident and agreed on all important points. Sis had worn his shades into class, something he had never done before. Told to remove them, he refused. The teacher—a young, aggressive woman—tried to jolly him out of his refusal; not succeeding, misunderstanding his quietness for pliability, she reached out and, laughing, snatched the glasses from his face. When she told me the story after lunch, deviating in only one crucial detail from the account I heard in the cafeteria, she had tears on her cheeks and unfeigned horror in her voice as she described the eyes her sudden action had uncovered.

The story the gang heard was not, according to the teacher, the event exactly as it happened. Snapper's faith in his friend had been more reliable than half a dozen eyewitness accounts. Sis had not struck her. He had caught her wrist with one hand, wrenched the glasses from her with the other, and run from the classroom. His hand grasping her wrist, her cry of shock and dismay at the sight of his eye— all could have contributed to the myth of assault. If anyone were guilty of assault, she said, it was she.

Before my meeting with the full faculty at the end of the day, I sought out Snapper to tell him that he had been right about his friend. His apparent relief helped me to repress the incident, thinking it all but closed, until I went to my car at 4:30 and found five quiet adolescents waiting for me on the steps of the school's unused entrance.

"You got time to talk?"

May can be hot in Washington. The day had been too long and too full. What I really wanted was to sit in my car, turn on the air-conditioner, and slowly freeze myself as I drove the Parkway to Baltimore.

"I've got time."

"We don't want to bother you none." The flat tone of Cleo's voice told me I hadn't covered up quickly enough.

"When you're bothering me I'll tell you. Let me take off my coat and I'll be all right."

I sat with my back against the door while Wentworth did the talking. He had been glad to hear that the teacher told the same story he had squeezed out of Sis. It was good he hadn't hit her and good she didn't claim to be hit, but the problem was worse than hitting any teacher. It was worse even than Sis's uncle punching him in the eye. Sis said that wasn't his uncle's way, and Wentworth believed him. It was *why* Sis had been hit that made the difference.

Sis's uncle had punched him in the eye because he was drunk and because Sis had flatly refused to stay with him after he sold his District poolroom in order to buy another down South. As Wentworth went on to report the reason for Sis's refusal, I had once again the feeling of being smothered by unreality. The heat, the long day, the demands of completing parallel and wildly different school years in Ann Arbor and Washington—I was light-headed and wet with perspiration as Wentworth reported that Sis wanted to stay in Washington *because he wanted to go to school.*

"You believe him?" I hadn't confronted Wentworth so directly since our first conversation in the cafeteria line. He was no longer a boy as he looked at me; then, slowly, he turned his head to look away from all of us, into the middle distance of Tenth Street.

"He didn't wanna tell me nothin'. Wouldn't of tole me that iff'n I didn't stay on him. Wanted to fight me and ever'-body. He *know* he ain't gettin' no more schoolin' do he go back with his uncle."

"You gotta talk to Sis's uncle." Snapper was speaking for all of them. That was why they had waited for me. I was supposed to fix everything.

"Not me!" I said instinctively. "Why should he listen to me?" I could see the two of us negotiating Sis's future at their kitchen table over beer and pretzels. The picture, never in focus, faded completely as I saw the anger and resentment on his uncle's face. Who was I to interfere?

"You the only one," said Cleo. "He ain't gonna listen to us but he listen to you." Then, looking into my thoughts as they retreated from my mouth: "Don't matter if you a white man. You the only one."

They had already worked out the initial part of the plan.

After three hours spent calming and sobering Sis, Wentworth had put him to bed and gone immediately to his own home to speak to his grandmother. Since his grandmother not only took care of the house and children while his mother worked, but also dominated the family, her permission was all he needed. She hadn't seen any reason why they couldn't take care of one more. If Sis wanted to live with them, they'd manage to find room for him. His need was bigger than theirs.

"His need is bigger" was the phrase Wentworth actually used in quoting his grandmother's reaction. I wrote it down that evening, for it seemed to me then the finest justification for charity I had ever heard. Now, five years later, with deeper experience of the extended family in black ghettos of urban America, I have come to realize that "his need is bigger" is more than a perfect statement. It is also an enviable standard for action which has all but disappeared from our suburban culture. Recognizing its absence and our loss, we who educate the impoverished child—especially those of us who, having attained middle-class insularity, now seek to make the impoverished black child inheritor of our isolation—would do well to embrace his values of the extended family even as we parade and extol our own singular values before him.

It was, after all, the influence of the extended family that prevailed upon Sis's uncle. We did not speak over beer and pretzels in his kitchen, but over racks of sticks and boxes of chalk in the storeroom-repair shop behind his poolhall. We spoke because the children's argument had proved unanswerable: I knew Sis and Wentworth; Sis's Uncle Mack knew me. My visits to his poolroom had recently expanded to include a game with him as well as the customary games with Snapper and Sis. We got along well, and therefore he might listen to me where no one else would gain either audience or credence.

I sat in silence, watching him work, not knowing where to begin my plea. We were in the repair shop together because I had brought my two-piece cue from Ann Arbor so that Snapper could see that I really owned one and Mack could repair the broken tip for me. When I reported the offer made by Wentworth's grandmother, he stopped sand-papering my cue and leaned on it for a long moment. Even the murmur and clink of voices and poolballs seemed momentarily to recede; then his hands started working the wood again and blind chance prevailed.

"He really want to go to school?"

"It's what he says. I believe him."

"His momma my sister."

"Dead?"

"Naw. Run off. Me'n' my woman took Sis. She been dead ten year."

"Wentworth's his friend. Wentworth's family will take care of him."

"It was on my mind. Promised my woman to see to him. Couldn't leave him lest I knowed he was looked after."

On the surface, there was no more to it than that. Beneath the vocal level of that brief and final conversation —Sis lived with Wentworth's family for two years until his uncle returned from the South—was the most important lesson I learned in my year as an alien visitor amongst the children and adults of Washington's black ghetto.

The lesson, hard learned, is equally difficult to teach. I am sure it is hard to learn because hundreds of urban school systems throughout the United States and a growing number in England have tried to comprehend it and most have failed. I am certain it is hard to teach because I have tried with remarkably small success to convey it to thousands of students and tens of thousands of teachers. The lesson is based on these observations and beliefs:

Isolation created by loss of the concept of extended family accounts for much of the consuming self-interest of predominantly white suburban families. This exclusive self-concern in turn accounts for the loss of traditional community involvement in educating the individual child. This is not to claim that the suburban community is less involved in the education of all its children than, say, the urban community of fifty years ago. It is, indeed, both more interested in that education and more knowledgable than any broadly based community in the history of Western civilization. What it is not, however, is *communally* interested in or identified with the success or failure of the individual child.

For *communal* read *familial*. The suburban family, enormously interested in its own, takes care of its own. If to do this it must also financially provide for the community's less fortunate few—then it says, resignedly, that the price of good education comes high. But not so high that the family can be expected to extend itself as well as its income to assure survival of the community's children. A moderate extension of income is self-protective; any extension of family is counter-productive, for it postpones or halts elimination of the unfit and leads to restriction of opportunity by glutting the market. Upon closer examination, an action that is apparently only counter-productive can be seen also to be self-destructive.

Values do not have to be assigned nor judgments made. The fact is that suburban white America has lost any sense of the extended family while urban black America would be lost without it. No choice is required of the child in either environment. He cannot have the world of his childhood in other shapes or fashions. He must take what he finds *and so must the adults who serve him*. Just as no teacher in suburbia can reasonably hope for communal support of the individual child, no urban teacher can expect to deal successfully with the individual child without dealing as well with his communal existence.

What this means for urban teachers and urban schools is the lesson so hard to teach and learn: The child who is raised with a sense of his collective existence cannot easily be influenced by an institution that ignores that existence. Even if a child does not find hostility to school in his community, he will be dissuaded of its relevance to him if he finds apathy or incomprehension. Since what is distant or mysterious to the community is veiled and opaque to the child, a primary and continuing effort of the school must be to remove the mystery of education for an uneducated community by making education's aims and methods comprehensible to that community.

The disastrous results of viewing the school as an institution physically located in the community but essentially separate from it, are clearly to be seen at all levels of education from elementary grades through the university. Just as the destructive and predictable anger of the surrounding community—from state legislators to local policemen—has vented itself at incalculable cost in five years of confrontation between various universities and their communities, so has the anger of epidemic incomprehension in the ghetto community virtually isolated public school education and rendered it impotent.

In my opinion, revitalization of the dead body of public education—now buried in the cemetery of the inner city—depends largely upon schools undertaking the activity which has proven least congenial to them in the past: opening themselves to the community. Instead of building their walls higher, they must open their doors wider to community participation. But the door must not be hinged to permit only an inward opening; if it is not an unmistakable invitation to entrance from both sides of the threshold, then it will lead to nothing. In the case of the teacher, the invitation must be a condition of employment as well as a humane command.

24

TO EXPECT MORE, to *demand* more of ourselves—the formula for personal success among the driven middle class has a variety of statements with a single conclusion: Within the elastic bounds of probability, you can do it if you set your mind to it. Expect it of yourself; demand it of yourself! You are the first and last barrier between yourself and. . . . "Success" is the word that usually completes the credo, though occasionally "happiness" or "satisfaction" are specified. Each is a separate facet of our indispensable belief in our capacity to exercise significant control over our lives.

If the school experience of impoverished black children can be characterized by a single condition, it is that it denies them the support of that indispensable belief. In an education where variability is infinite and certainty minute, the one reliable factor is the child's belief that he controls little and can accomplish less. In holding this view of himself he proves an apt pupil to his teachers, who teach him to know himself as powerless and incompetent. Of all the means employed to rob children of their essential belief in themselves, none is more insidious or more effective than the outrage of minimal demand.

In their three-year study of five high schools, one in Ann Arbor and four in other communities in southeastern Michigan, Professors Robert D. Vintner and Rosemary C. Sarri of the University of Michigan confirmed both the existence and effectiveness of the method for destroying children I have called *minimal demand*. The following paragraphs are taken from a two-part interview with Vintner and Sarri published in the *Ann Arbor News* in November of 1966:

Mrs. Sarri noted "a strong tendency by teachers, counselors, and administrators to regard students from working-class homes as less capable than students from upper- and middle-class backgrounds.

"This results in a disproportionate number of working-class students being placed in the various non-college-preparatory curricula, regardless of their I.Q. scores, reading abilities as reflected on tests or other objective criteria.

"The general (curriculum) student thus starts discouraged," Mrs. Sarri said. "Once in the general curriculum, students are further discouraged by the discovery that different grading standards exist among the curricula, with teachers and administrators applying a different [lower] set of expectations to the general curriculum than they do to the college-preparatory curriculum.

"The secondary school, unlike the university, feels it has a social control responsibility as well as an educational responsibility," she said. "Since working-class students are assumed by school personnel to have fewer advantages at home and to present greater behavior problems, they are also assumed to have less inherent ability.

"Students frequently are shunted into the general curriculum to avoid potential behavior problems in the college preparatory classes before they have had a chance to demonstrate whether they would in fact create behavior problems.

"This attitude contributes to the very behavior it is supposed to avoid."

. . . .

The researchers found a . . . significantly higher [dropout rate] in the general curriculum than in the college preparatory curriculum: "The differential we found had little or no relation to the native talents and abilities of the students," Vintner says. "All of the pupils studied were capable of completing high school and began their careers motivated to do so."

. . . .

At Ann Arbor High, the report says, the general curriculum "was viewed to be of low status by teachers and pupils alike. In fact, pupils reported that they often hid their books so that others would not know that they were in the general curriculum."

The report also shows that students in the general curriculum receive lower grades regardless of their I.Q. and social levels. This is "a result of different grading standards between the two curricula, apparently with an arbitrary devaluation of performance within the general curriculum."

Though Vintner and Sarri do not suggest an immediate cause for the effect of "arbitrary devaluation of performance"—the original cause being the assumption that general students "have less inherent ability"—that immediate cause is clearly the minimal demand which teachers are aware of making. Since they know only too well that they have asked for little and accepted less, they cannot bring themselves to recognize the performance of hopeless children with rewards appropriate to promising students. No more vicious cycle of bad conscience and worse action can readily be imagined.

My opinion of the practice of minimal demand, as so many opinions I now hold of education in America, owes much of its expanded shape to the five children who helped me see it broadly. Unlike other lessons they taught me, this one had a painfully sharp and cutting edge:

I had been asked during the winter to describe the project at Garnet-Patterson to a meeting of elementary teachers, but various conflicting engagements on both sides caused postponement of the meeting until late spring. The timing was unfortunate because of my commitment to Cleo and her boys. As our year together drew to its close, we found ourselves with several promises on both sides unfulfilled. One of mine had been the promise to take them to a poolroom with a billiard table—Mack had only pool tables —so that they could see how the game was played. It was Snapper the pool player who put together my obligation to make a speech with his desire to see a billiard game.

"Gonna be June and we ain't done no billiards," he said to me wistfully one Friday afternoon. "And you can't do none next week on accounta them meetin's."

I had just been explaining that next week would be lost to us because I had to attend long meetings after school on both afternoons. I was unhappily aware that only three weeks were left to me of their companionship. For the first time I realized that I did not want the year to end.

"We could play a little billiards after my meetings next Thursday. Both of them are here at school. If you can wait until five o'clock. . . ."

"Can't do it, man." Rubbergut, unexpectedly. "Me'n' him gonna be gone all day."

"Yeah," Snapper confirmed reluctantly, "we gonna visit our grampa in Virginia Wednesday afternoon. Ain't comin' back till Friday mornin'." Then, suddenly, his face alight with the inspiration: "If'n you got the time, we could maybe take you in and do some billiards after."

"Take me in?"

"Yeah. You know, man, catch your act."

And that's how five junior high school students came to be sitting at the rear of the auditorium when I told several hundred elementary school teachers the story of Jonathan and the lever. Jonathan was one of twenty children, all four years old, in a nursery school near a large university; I was the lever:

As all other graduate students supported solely by the G.I. Bill, I needed extra income. Being a graduate student in English and therefore unskilled labor, the best-paying job I could find was employment as a "male presence" in a nursery school. What the ladies who owned the school wanted was a male counterbalance for the female weight which bears upon very young children in school and home. Since what I wanted was survival, I accepted the job with gratitude and disbelief: Did they really intend to pay me two dollars an hour for playing with little children?

They did, but the job was only nineteen-twentieths possible. The twentieth part's name was Jonathan, who was like the other nineteen children in the privileged home he came from, and unlike them in that he was a spastic. Jonathan's spasticity took three apparent forms, two of which primarily concerned only the child and his family: His right leg from the hip girdle down was of no use to him, causing him to depend upon a single crutch to substitute for the useless leg. And his hands were of little use to him near his body, though he was surprisingly dextrous and manipulative with his arms extended.

Neither of these manifestations of his spasticity was the cause of his severe problem with his peer group in the nursery school. His crutch, in fact, was an object of some envy because its rubber tip, combined with his rubber-soled shoes, enabled him to walk *up* the slide of the sliding board.

What no one envied, however, was the uncontrollable drool-
ing with which birth damage had afflicted him. In spite of
the wad of Kleenex which his mother stuffed in his shirt
pocket every morning and which every adult who knew him
would use to wipe him dry, his mouth, chin, and shirtfront
were constantly wet.

Perhaps everyone who has dealt with physical abnormali-
ties in relation to normal children knows how such children
react to a Jonathan. But I had no recent experience of little
children and no experience at all of damaged children. Consequently I was astounded and sickened by the treatment he
received at the hands of his peers.

Two-thirds of the children simply ignored him. If he came
to join their group or individual play, they either pretended
he wasn't there or abandoned whatever they were doing in
order to avoid his company. But they were the more secure
ones. The less secure, the ones least happy with themselves,
found Jonathan intolerable. "Go away!" they would whisper
or shout. "You're dirty. Dirty, dirty, dirty Jonathan! Go
away! We don't want to play with you!"

Few adults can witness any child abused and not inter-
vene. When the child is as unfortunate and defenseless as
Jonathan, the abuse is unbearable. At the end of three futile
mornings of intervention and rebuff, I was defeated. When
the children had gone home, I sought out my employers to
quit my job.

"Don't leave because of Jonathan," they said. I realized
that they had seen more of me in those three mornings than
I had of them.

"I'm sorry," I said, and I was, "but you need somebody
better trained than I am. If you want me to, I'll help you
look for a man who's doing his graduate work in child psy-
chology. Maybe he'll know how to help Jonathan. I've tried
and I can't."

"Neither can we," they said, and went on to tell me about their failed efforts of the past month. Jonathan was an experiment. His mother had prevailed upon them to take the child on a trial basis. She was an intelligent, realistic woman who knew too much about other children's problems with her son to expect success at the nursery school. What she had hoped for was exactly what the school had been able to provide: a month's respite for her, supervised activity for Jonathan, and an opportunity for him to experience and perhaps adjust to the treatment of his peers. Protected as he was at home, she felt he now needed some portion of exterior reality to prepare him for the inevitable cruelties of elementary school.

Nursery school had provided him with that reality. Both women were profoundly disturbed by their ineffective efforts on his behalf, but they did not have my option of quitting. Since the school was their livelihood, they would stay and Jonathan would go at the end of the week. Knowing that, would I like to remain?

I would, but I felt as defeated as they did. We sat and talked quietly, depressed by our inability to meet a child's desperate need. They recounted the various stratagems and devices they had employed in his behalf. During our hour's conversation I asked an undirected question: How had the children reacted to their explanation of Jonathan's affliction? I had nothing in mind as a sequel to the question, whatever its answer. Perhaps because my thoughts were in total pause, perhaps because I felt such despair at our failure—whatever the reason, I heard and understood not only the intent but also the implication of their words. For the first time, I was aware of thinking about children as people instead of possessions. Seen from that viewpoint, their answer was extraordinary.

If extraordinary in my view, their answer is well-founded

and thoroughly unremarkable in the world of childhood education. Their answer to my question began with a question: Explanation of Jonathan's affliction? To four-year-olds? One could explain that sort of thing to little children for days on end, they said, and it would remain a mystery to them. After all, children don't need to understand Jonathan with their heads; they need to understand him with their hearts. What *we* need to do—what we've failed to do—is to get them to *feel* for Jonathan. You can't expect a four-year-old to understand with more than his heart.

I listened and realized that I knew they were wrong. How or why I knew it, I couldn't be sure. Nor were they speaking of any children I had ever known. Years later, after coming to know children and their teachers (and *their* teachers) better—or at least professionally, which may not be the same thing at all—I recognized the children they were describing. They were describing the depersonalized infant of childhood education, the diminished reflection of fearful adults who have canvassed their own disabilities and then made programs for children disabled like themselves.

What they were speaking of were children as they believed them to be, not as they knew them to be. Operating from a concept of the child rather than from his reality, they had predetermined the child's capacities and then discovered those capacities to be just as they had thought. Strengthened by this remarkable coincidence, they had proceeded to define a creature incapable of any but the least thought and action. Which of course was precisely what was then expected of him, since no other demands could reasonably be made.

As I listened to what I did not believe, I came to see clearly what I did believe: that four-year-old children must not be spared the human requirement of accepting a

Jonathan. Let their thought processes remain their own, as inscrutable before the act as after. Understanding in our terms need not be demanded of them; only acceptance. Given the weight of rejection rather than incomprehension as the mass to be moved, all Jonathan needed to move it was a place to stand and a lever long enough. Given a little time, I thought I could supply him with both.

I tried to fit a simple problem with an equally simple solution: Since I was the only available creature who played like a man, most of the children in the nursery coveted me for a playmate. Little boys courted me; little girls flirted with me; but only Jonathan had me. Wherever I was and whatever I did, he was there doing it with me. When I read stories to the children, he sat closest to me and I often began by reading to him alone. When he played, we played. Sandbox or fingerpaints, we were as near to being inseparable companions as either of us could bear. And the other children got the message: If you wanted me, you had to take him. What's more, you had to talk to him and about him.

Jonathan was a bright child whose resourceful mother had helped him to understand the physical fact of himself. In a small shower of spittle, drawing in the sand, he could explain what had happened to him. I have no idea what the children understood when he told them he had lost air while he was being born because the cord had come out first and they couldn't let him be born the quick way. Did they see some childish image of a balloon on a long string with air escaping? What does it matter, so long as they understood that Jonathan *must be accepted*? What does conceptual thought matter when realized action is needed? Our confusion of the relationship between the two, which amounts to imposing our own incapacitating needs upon children, has led us to the dreadful practice of minimal demand.

Jonathan attended nursery school for the entire four months of the spring term. Certainly not all of the children accepted him; perhaps not one of them accepted him fully. But that does not matter either. What does matter is that a community of nineteen normal children found a place for one abnormal child because it was inconceivable that less should be demanded of them.

The speech was a long one, followed by questions that were sharp and strenuous. Afterward, as I drove away with my five companions, I was grateful for their silence. I felt spent, relieved to have only a few games of billiards between the end of the week and a plane ride back to Michigan. My relief, however, was premature, for once again Cleo and her boys confounded my expectations.

25

"YOU KNOW, about that Jonathan—all them teachers teach in elementary school?"

"The ones at the meeting?"

"Yeah. Teachers you tole about Jonathan."

"Yes. Kindergarten through sixth. All of them."

Uncle Wiggly was first to break the silence. Until he began his question about Jonathan and then veered off to ask about the teachers, I had been concentrating on driving in five o'clock traffic and thinking about playing billiards. Because Jonathan's story was not one that I told often, and because I saw no particular application of its lesson to older children, I was surprised at Uncle Wiggly's reference to it. But before I could question him, I found myself being questioned by Snapper who had obviously been waiting for someone else to broach the subject:

"What happen to him?"

"I don't know."

"How come you don't know? Didn't see him no more?"

"No. I only worked in the nursery school for one semester. I meant to find out about him but I never did."

"Nothin' to find out. He make it big." Wentworth's first contribution. Cleo was listening intently, while Rubbergut's attention was elsewhere.

"What makes you so sure?" I was becoming aware that Rubbergut and I were the only absentees. The rest were deeply engaged by thoughts of Jonathan and by something they hadn't yet managed to convey.

"Oh, he make it. Always have somebody lookin' out for him. Don't need to worry none about him."

Of all the judgments I might have anticipated from Wentworth and the others—who made their agreement obvious—this was the one I least expected. Something very like animosity gave an edge to their tone. I was amazed; perhaps I had misunderstood—"Being spastic is pretty tough. No matter who looks out for you."

"Don't have to be spastic in our school. How come you don't tell about Jonathan to ever'body?"

After a year's initiation I didn't often lose the thread of conversation so completely. Uncle Wiggly, Snapper, and Wentworth were talking about the same thing and I didn't know what it was. They were so tuned in to each other that they were asking each other's questions. I felt like odd man out at a seance. "To everybody? Who do you mean?"

"Teachers at Garnet-Patterson. Teachers at that school where you comes from."

"How do you know I don't?"

" 'At blue book don't say so."

"And teachers at Garnet-Patterson don't act like you tole 'em." Cleo had completed Wentworth's thought. Jonathan's story had powerfully affected four of my five companions, but I had no idea what its affecting elements were for them. What Cleo said was perfectly true—I hadn't told the junior high school faculty about Jonathan because the moral of the story seemed appropriate to teachers of younger children. Cleo was intelligent and perceptive, but she wasn't omniscient. What did she mean when she said that the teachers didn't *act* like I'd told them? I had never seen a single spastic child in the school. Was she referring to one or more who had already graduated or dropped out?

"Ever' year the Year of the Dog in *that* school." Some of the same words she had used months ago, only this time the word *that* loaded with unutterable disdain. And this time we had no chorus of barking boys to lighten the condemnation, to make the truth more bearable. I was too tired to cover my own disappointment and sense of loss.

"Hasn't it been better this year? I mean, with all the changes and everything." I finished lamely, embarrassed by what I heard myself asking for. What I wanted was their praise, their testimonial to the success of my theories and methods. What I wanted was nothing less than their gratitude. Hadn't I come from Ann Arbor to Washington for two days almost every week for nine months? Hadn't I . . . hadn't we together . . . what was left to say? It was the Year of the Dog.

"Sure it been better this year," said Snapper, assuming the shifting mantle of my champion. "It been *best* this year," he added, looking around at the others as though daring any one to gainsay the truth.

"Sure it has," echoed Wentworth, "sure it has."

I felt shamed as I understood how cleanly I had excised and disposed of the growth of criticism even before I knew whether it was malignant or benign. It had been offered for my examination and I had responded by throwing it away in ignorance and fear. I tried to retrieve it:

"Listen, Cleo—what did you mean when you said the teachers at Garnet-Patterson didn't act like I told them about Jonathan? You're right. I never did. And I never told the teachers at the school in Michigan either. But how did you know?

I had asked the question of Cleo, but I had been unable to look at her as I spoke because traffic took my attention. When I caught her eyes in the mirror, she looked away. The silence in the car was oppressive by the time she brought herself to respond. I think the answer was as difficult for her to speak as it was for me to hear.

"Ain't downin' you none," she began, almost reflectively. "Done all you could. And we got pret' near ever'body usin' all them newspapers and ever'thin' else." Another long pause, then gently—"But it ain't comin' to much."

"Ain't bad to be readin' them good things in class," observed the same Wentworth who six months ago would read nothing in class, "but mostly 'at's all we does. Sits and reads newspapers and everything. Don't learn nothin'."

I have tried several times with no success to reproduce that conversation. Perhaps the reason for my failure lies equally in the children's indirectness for fear of hurting my feelings and in my own remembered discomfort as I listened to them. Though I cannot now repeat the words they used, I will never forget their substance. The lesson they taught me has significantly altered my understanding of public education as it affects the life of the impoverished child.

Their lesson was simple, clear, and based upon a devastating accusation: In equal portion with Jonathan's peers, they shared in and suffered from the destruction of minimal demand. No, it wasn't just the dumbhead classes. Cleo and Wentworth could give sure witness to that since they were in top and bottom classes in the ninth grade. Though Wentworth had both decided and proceeded "to do it different" during the course of the year, his decision had come too late to affect his placement in the grade. Smarthead and dumbhead classes were engaged in equally rapid pursuit of the same thing: nothing. Empty days, nothing asked and nothing given.

Then, for me, the worst part of their indictment. Though school was more bearable for most bottom classes since introduction of my program, and better especially during the second semester after its general acceptance in the school, the days had actually gotten worse for top classes. She would have told me anyhow, Cleo said, but my story about Jonathan had made her think of it in a different way. Before my program came to the school, bad old teachers followed bad old books and you could learn something if you wanted to. Then the program put a lot of new things in place of old things and bad teachers just gave up. Couldn't use the old stuff; wouldn't use the new stuff. Just gave it out and then gave up. No more to tell than that.

There is, unfortunately, much more to tell than that. After telling the tale of the visiting expert who didn't know that some weak teachers would surrender everything in the face of change—not only bad methods but *all* methods; if they couldn't do it their way, they wouldn't do it any way— there is the more important story to tell of weak and strong teachers alike who have given up far more than methods, far more than they have the right to renounce. They are the ones who have surrendered their expectations and given up hope for their students. The cycle of despair which such action generates is as easy to observe as it is difficult to interrupt.

After being led by the hand to understand in that May afternoon what I should have seen for myself long before, I have had the lesson my friends taught me confirmed again and again in these intervening years: The inadequate intellectual and emotional demands we make upon infants and small children are not unique to that age. Far from ending in early childhood, they continue to be the educational substance we feed to older children and adolescents. Perhaps the privileged child survives such malnourishment, but our inner-city schools are full of children of all ages who suffer from a famine more debilitating than most poverty can bring. According to the system which incarcerates them, they also have in common—whatever their apparent intellect—a diminished capacity to learn.

Just as the moral of Jonathan's story is applicable to a far greater spectrum of age, ability, and privilege than that found in a nursery school, so are the findings of Professors Vintner and Sarri relevant to a system for broader than five senior high schools. If insufficient demands are the general rule in American public education, they are the specific rule in educating the impoverished child. As Vintner and Sarri point out, "Since working-class students are assumed by school personnel to have fewer advantages at home and to present greater behavior problems, they are also assumed to have less inherent ability." Like guilt, once the assumption of small ability is made, the fact is inevitable.

26

WE HAD OUR farewell party on a Friday evening in the middle of June. The party honored and mourned various leave-takings, for more important changes than my departure were happening in Cleo's gang. Snapper and Rubbergut had returned from visiting their grandfather in Virginia to report that they would soon be moving back to Alabama where their family had a farm. They didn't want to go, but nobody had asked them what they wanted and their grampa was no man to argue with.

Not only were Snapper and Rubbergut leaving the group, but Uncle Wiggly was a likely defector as well. His mother was talking about moving in with his aunt, her sister, in order to cut the expenses of maintaining two households. Since his aunt had the larger apartment and lived in southeast Washington, Uncle Wiggly didn't expect to last out the summer on Tenth Street.

And, finally, by unanimous approval we had extended invitations to Sis and his Uncle Mack. Mack would be leaving at the end of June, and our party seemed like the right time for everybody to say good-bye to him. Since the man who was buying the poolroom was spending most of June learning the trade, Mack would be able to get away for a few hours on Friday evening.

By unspoken agreement, Cleo and Wentworth had become co-leaders of the gang during the spring, and the party was their joint farewell to the others as well as to the year of our friendship. Both of them would graduate in a week from Garnet-Patterson, and next autumn would go up the hill to the high school. Both knew, I think, that the gang would not survive even if Snapper, Rubbergut, and Uncle Wiggly were to remain in the old neighborhood. We all wanted a special party to mark the end of many things.

In anticipation of that June evening, I made various references to our January journey to the University of Maryland and our dinner in College Park. Each time I referred to it, I managed to include a reminder that I had been their guest for dinner and they had yet to give me opportunity to repay. On the Friday after my speech to the elementary teachers, when we were on our way to Mack's poolroom, Wentworth smiled obliquely across the width of the front seat and told me that I "didn't have to work on setting us up no more."

"For what?" I asked, pretending ignorance.

"You knows for what," he replied, smiling more broadly. After that, only minor negotiations were necessary to agree on the evening, the guest list, and the division of financial responsibility. I would pay for the meal and they would leave the tip. Solomon's justice could not have arrived at a more equitable division.

My last Thursday and Friday in Washington actually began on Wednesday night, for I had Thursday appointments too early to take the morning plane. When I entered my hotel room, I found an enormous floral bouquet in a vase and a packet of Callard and Bowser's licorice toffee lying in front of it on the dresser. The flowers could have been from anybody, but the flowers and licorice together could only have been from Cleo and her boys. Whenever we were together and stopped for candy, I bought this particular toffee if I could get it. And once on a dull winter's day I had told them if I couldn't be a teacher I might like to move out West and become a flower farmer. The idea of farming flowers had fascinated them and often had entered our conversations of the late winter and spring.

I brought the empty licorice packet with me the next morning to the hotel lobby. I came down earlier than usual because I didn't want my guests to arrive before me, but the six were already waiting in two overstuffed sofas in the middle of the lobby. "What time did you all get up?" I asked.

"Didn't go to bed," answered Wentworth. "Afraid we gonna have trouble gettin' him up, so we was pinchin' him all night to keep him awake." The *him* he nodded his head toward was Sis, who grinned and pointed to the licorice box I was carrying.

"Ain't much for breakfast," he said.

"Man has to make do with what he's got," I answered. "Flowers taste like flowers."

"You like 'em?" Only Rubbergut would have asked me directly. His simplicity often made things easier for all of us.

"Best flowers I ever tasted," I said. All six had smiles of satisfaction on their faces as we entered the dining room for breakfast.

Breakfast on Thursday morning and dinner on Friday evening of our last two days together—the two meals were no accident. In a hundred different comments during the year they had told me that their rarest pleasure was enough good food. Uncle Wiggly's impressions of our afternoon and evening at the University of Maryland had reduced them-

selves over a period of several months to memories of all
that soft grass to walk on and all that good food to eat. If
he mentioned the two once, he spoke of them a dozen times.
In recalling that meal as the highest point of our visit, he
reflected the unanimous feeling of the group.

We met at my hotel for breakfast because our Friday
evening party required planning and Thursday morning
before school was the only time we could find to be together.
Of the seven of us, at least three understood that the meeting was something less than a necessity, but neither Wentworth nor Cleo was any more likely than I to forego it
because of that. As for who would pay, I was never allowed
to buy the group anything, not even candy or ice cream.
My explanation of a few unspent dollars in my federal contract had been considered and found acceptable as the
source of support for our breakfast.

Had the life of our Friday evening party depended upon
the planning accomplished at Thursday's breakfast, it would
have been stillborn. Only one of the experiences we shared
during the preceding nine months had the paralyzing effect
of that hotel dining room on my companions. The mounted
policeman on the Mall in front of the National Gallery had
been almost too much for them to deal with, but they had
managed. They never managed to cope with that dining
room at all. Six children sat, ate, stared, and departed while
one adult began conversations that invariably turned into
monologues.

Because we would not have a great deal of time, and
because I thought it would make the experience easier for
them to enjoy, I had inquired about their tastes beforehand
and ordered accordingly. The table at which we were seated
soon had seven large glasses of orange juice placed upon it;
Uncle Wiggly was flabbergasted:

"How they know we want orange juice?"

"I told them."

"How you know?"

"You told me. Remember when I asked you last week about what you'd like to have for breakfast?"

"Yeah. . . ." But he wasn't really convinced. Who ever heard of a place where they had your food waiting for you? It was a wary, watchful group that sat at the table with me.

If the orange juice was hard for Uncle Wiggly to account for, the main course was beyond belief. When we had talked about breakfast, Rubbergut had dreamt aloud about a plate of hotcakes with two fried eggs on top, all covered with syrup and surrounded by links of pork sausage. No, he had replied with considerable dignity to Snapper's taunt, he had never had himself anything like that, but he would know what to do with it if he did. The others—even Snapper—had agreed that Ruggergut's vision was beautiful to behold.

When the vision became seven platefuls of reality, it was still beautiful but it was almost too much to behold. If one meal in their collective lives had amounted to nothing, it was breakfast. School lunches and working adults' requirements for supper had caused them to be passingly familiar with enough food at noon and evening meals, but a full breakfast was an experience reserved for people you saw on television or read about in books. Six wide-eyed children stared at their breakfasts and might have been staring yet had I not begun to cut and chew with obvious satisfaction.

"Gov'min' sure got a lot of money." Uncle Wiggly's comment, directed to nobody, as he watched the waiter remove our empty plates from the table.

"Worser ways to spend it." Rubbergut, laconically, from behind his third cup of coffee. Only good fortune had kept me from specifying a glass of milk for everyone when I had arranged our breakfast with the assistant manager. All six drank great quantities of coffee with their breakfasts; all thought that my pot of tea or the milk I diffidently suggested were odd breakfast drinks, to say the least.

"*Worse*, not *worser*. Ain't no such word." The first time in nine months that I had heard one child correct the language of another. Wentworth's correction of Rubbergut was gentler than Rubbergut's retort.

"Who say? My momma say *worser* and she oughta know!"

"Ain't no such word, is there?" Wentworth appealed the question to me. It wasn't an appeal I was anxious to arbitrate.

"No," I said, "there isn't." If I had learned anything during our time together, it was that equivocation was always transparent to their eyes. If you told them as much of the truth as you knew, they could usually arrange it to be bearable. Half-truths or well-meant lies were anathema, and I had to overcome my instincts in order to stop myself from dealing in them. Once having told the truth, however, charity was not only permissable but required: "But everybody makes up words like *worser* because they sound right. That's one way we get new words in our language. Maybe someday *worser* will be in the dictionary just because so many people say it."

"But *right now* it's wrong?" Wentworth wouldn't have pushed it that far; it was Rubbergut who sensed equivocation.

"Yes."

"Anyway, I ain't gonna tell her." Rubbergut might never be president, as Snapper had said, but he would be a good man.

"You made the reservation for tomorrow night?" Even shared leadership with Wentworth hadn't displaced Cleo's sure guidance when difficult corners needed turning.

"Yes," I replied, "for eight of us."

"Mack gonna come?" This to Sis.

"Sure. Been talkin' 'bout it all week." Before Sis could get out the rest of the words his mind was framing, the assistant manager was upon us.

"Everything all right, Professor?"

"Fine. Just fine."

"How about you youngsters? I'll bet you've never been inside a place like this before."

Not in a hotel like this, I thought, not in 1966 in the capital city of the United States. When I arranged the meal with him he had been interested and efficient. After I told him I was having six thirteen- and fourteen-year-olds to breakfast, he had gone so far as to instruct the doorman to usher my guests inside and to make them feel welcome when they came. Now his eyes, his face, and his words told all seven of us what he was seeing as he looked at our table.

It would be some small satisfaction now to report how we put him in his place. In fact, we said and did nothing. For all of us, I think, that beaming ass represented all we had fought and perhaps all we would not overcome in the world of fools and bigots. Our small satisfaction at seeing him leave us with a thinner smile than when he came, is all too small when measured against the hurt he left behind.

27

FRIDAY NIGHT brought a huge rainstorm that inundated the northwestern part of the city. Torrents of mud and debris poured into Connecticut Avenue from every side street; buses stalled in deep water, passengers joined pedestrians in wading on submerged sidewalks, and taxi drivers refused to accept fares to or from inner-city areas where flooding was worst. Just as the rain began I entered Harvey's Restaurant on Connecticut Avenue next door to the Mayflower Hotel. I was an hour early for my reservation because I wanted to be sure that the headwaiter and waiter perfectly understood our arrangements. Both were known to me as I was to them, and both were black men, but one assistant manager had been enough. This time I wanted no surprised expression on anyone's face.

With everything done and forty-five minutes remaining, I found that I couldn't enjoy my newspaper. The rain was falling unabated—if anything, harder than before—and I was thinking of six children and one adult trying to get two cabs in that neighborhood in this weather. The more I thought about it, the more improbable it seemed. If the gathering crowd in front of the Mayflower couldn't command enough transportation, what chance had my friends? The blowing rain had soaked my pants to the knees by the time I retrieved my car from the Mayflower Garage and drove away from Connecticut Avenue toward Tenth Street.

A ten-minute drive became forty interminable minutes of avoiding stalled cars and buses, and negotiating corners where stoplights were either stuck on red or not operating at all. As the time for our dinner party drew closer and I was still blocks away from Mack's apartment, where the seven had planned to meet before going to Harvey's, I realized how futile my journey was. Even if I found them at the apartment—if my car didn't stall or smash before I reached them—I couldn't risk maiming us all with another wild dash, even if the dash was a crawl, through those flooded and perilous streets.

When I drove up in front of the house where Mack had his apartment, the rain was so heavy that I couldn't see the front door. Five more minutes brought no relief in the downpour and no sign of movement from the house. If they were there and had seen me, I was sure they would have found a way to make themselves known. I slid across the front seat, opened the curb-side door, and raced up the walk to the house. Five boys, a girl, and a man burst out laughing as I pressed my soaked and steaming body into the small, packed hallway.

"Didn't know it was a swimmin' party," Snapper said, backing away from my wetness. "Anyways, you forgot to bring your suit."

"Get outta the man's way." It was Mack, already opening the door to his apartment. "He need a towel wors'n he need a wise mouth."

They had ordered two cabs for 6:30, fifteen minutes after the rains began. It made no difference that they had ordered the taxis at four o'clock. Because all cabs were staying out of the area until the rain stopped, their order had remained unfilled and they had been unable to find a cruising cab on the Avenue. As I dried my head and face to the point where I could see around me, I realized that Mack's trouser legs from the knee to the cuff were as wet as mine.

"Swimming with your pants on?" I asked.

"Sure," he smiled, "with a raincoat and umbrella too. Couldn't get a cab no way."

"Could now," said Rubbergut from his place beside the window. "It done stopped."

It had. The streets were awash but no more rain was falling. We walked out onto the stoop to get a better view of the aftermath. The gutter on the other side of the street was a wild river; oddly, the gutter nearest us had only several inches of water. Rubbergut, on closer terms with his belly than the rest of us, led the way:

"Ain't nothin' to keep us back now, is they?"

I was a long time answering because that forty-minute drive had jangled my nerves, but the rain had stopped. The sky looked less threatening, and my car was parked at the curb. "Nothing," I agreed, and we packed ourselves into the car.

Five blocks later we stopped for a light and the car stopped for the night. Having had enough water already, perhaps it had a foreboding of the deluge to come. Just as we pushed it against the curb, the rain began again and we repacked ourselves into its interior. At first the fall was very light and the motor made promising sounds. Soon the rain was heavier and the motor made no sounds at all. To compound our troubles, we had the choice of smothering with the windows closed or drowning with them open. We must have all come to the same conclusion at about the same time, but it was Mack who supplied us with a destination:

"No use to sittin' here," he announced. "Rain's warm and a little water never hurt nobody. Got plenty of TV dinners back to my place. What d'you say?"

We had our farewell party at Mack's place. The rain was warm but it was also wet. After five blocks of a downpour so dense that we had trouble crossing intersections because we could not see across the street, we may have been the eight wettest creatures in the District of Columbia. But Mack had more than TV dinners and towels. He also had an old trunk full of one of the largest collections of GI underwear, trousers, and shirts that I have ever seen outside of the Quartermaster Corps. As he said, he hadn't spent four years as an army supply sergeant for nothing.

I sat idly watching the rain through the front window while Mack and Sis got the dinners and Cleo put other necessities on the small table. Wentworth was standing behind me, going through the pockets of his sodden jacket, when I heard him laugh and saw his hand thrust a piece of paper over my shoulder. Since it was folded and soggy with rain, I began to open it carefully.

"Don't need to be careful," Wentworth said as he watched my hands. "It ain't worth nothin' to nobody."

As he said that, the paper came unfolded in my fingers. On it was Rob's full name, address, and telephone number at the University of Maryland. I don't know how long I sat there staring at it, the year evoked by a small piece of paper, until Cleo put a tray with a TV dinner on my khaki-covered knees and a beer in my free hand. It was a wonderful party.

Epilogue

MY LAST MEETING with the Garnet-Patterson faculty was as brief as others had been prolonged. I spoke for a few minutes, summarizing what I thought had been accomplished and what remained to be done in the teaching of willing literacy within the school. Whatever I said may have been as incoherent as it was unplanned because I was distracted by the scene before me. For the first and only time that year the thin, hard line of my implacable antagonists had dispersed, its ten-odd members having spread themselves indiscriminately throughout the room. What I had been unable to accomplish with nine months of intense effort, the end of the year had brought about with ease.

When I had promised to return for several one-day visits during the next academic year, and received the faculty's thanks from both principal and English chairman, I thought my working year in Washington was done. I had already begun to gather my papers and to shake the proffered hands of front-row faculty, when one of the teachers stood up at her seat and asked to be heard. Her prescient, passionate words have sounded in my ears over these intervening years:

"We've made a lot of changes around here. Some of us swear we're never going to go back to teaching the way we did. We say we'll never use the old textbooks again, and we mean it. But what will we do when we can't get newspapers, magazines, and paperbacks? What will we do when there's no one coming around every week to support us and no one to get us money for all these new materials? I wish you'd tell me that."

Some of the teachers had been standing while she spoke. When she paused, they quietly sat down. Even the principal, who had already reached the hall, came back into the room and sat by the door. I was searching for a reply when she continued:

"I don't mean to sound like I'm not happy with what we've done. I am, and so are a lot of others. There's some who wouldn't be happy with anything, but they're not the problem. The problem is . . . I mean, we've all seen a lot of new programs come and go. We don't want to see this one end up like all the others. But it will. I know it will."

It did. Slowly, perhaps inevitably, it ended up "like all the others." I returned to the school four times during the 1966–67 academic year, meeting twice with English and social studies teachers and twice with the full faculty. The further we got into the new year, the more bland and soporific our meetings became. I began to feel like a minister called upon for a eulogy at the graveside of a stranger. In the burial of "English In Every Classroom" at Garnet-Patterson, however, we reversed the usual procedure by first interring the spirit while leaving the body for later attention. By year's end, the spirit was covered with dust and the body had begun to decay.

One important factor in the program's decline was the departure of every member of Cleo's original gang. Only Sis remained, but he had never been a part of the underground effort to change the teaching of literacy in the school. Uncle Wiggly was living in southeastern Washington, Snapper and Rubbergut had moved to Alabama, while Cleo and Wentworth had gone up the hill to high school. Even though many of the troops they had employed in their original battles were still fighting rearguard actions, the captains had departed the field. A leaderless campaign for pleasure-in-literacy ground slowly to a halt in the school.

I never saw the three younger boys again. On my first two visits during that second year, I met after school with Cleo, Wentworth, and Sis and the four of us went to Mack's former poolroom where Sis and I shot a couple of games while Cleo and Wentworth provided us with an audience. On my third visit, as on my fourth, I met only with Cleo and Wentworth and we did not go to the poolroom. When I asked about Sis, Wentworth said he wasn't feeling so good and wouldn't be with us that afternoon. A few minutes later, not looking at my face, he told me that the real reason Sis wasn't feeling so good was because the new owner had made it clear to him that no honkey, whether a friend of Mack's or not, was welcome in his poolroom. Sis hadn't wanted to be the one to tell me.

On my fourth visit, in the late spring of 1967, the three of us had supper together. We talked a little about the future and a lot about the past. The year had been a good one for both of them. Cleo, influenced by her proficiency in the sciences, had changed her mind about becoming a medical secretary and had decided to be a nurse; Wentworth, put in a smarthead class for the first time in his life, had changed his mind about a lot of things. Next year would see him still in school though he had long since obtained his mother's and grandmother's permission to leave school after his sixteenth birthday. There were, he said, still some things he didn't know about, which was why he would stay on for graduation.

Uncle Wiggly had come back to visit a couple of times,

but it was a long journey from southeastern Washington to Tenth Street and they didn't expect to see him again. Sis had stopped drinking entirely because Wentworth's grandmother wouldn't stand for it, and he was going to be promoted to the ninth grade. Both were considerable victories, and Wentworth thought maybe Sis had made it. Even if his uncle returned and Sis went to live with him again, he was likely to be all right. The note of pride in Wentworth's voice, when he talked about Sis, said as much about him as it did about his friend.

Yes, they both knew what was happening to "English In Every Classroom" at Garnet-Patterson. I wasn't either surprised or disappointed, was I? Cleo was amazed that I was feeling a little of both. Hadn't I said that the reason for putting the program in Garnet-Patterson was to show that it would work in a public school the same way it worked in a reform school? That's what I said and that's what I'd done. Nobody expected it to last; after all, she said, nothing ever does.

Part Two

A few days after returning from a conference in England on the special language of unsuccessful children, I received a letter from a teacher in New York who had requested and received materials on the education of the impoverished child. Her letter ended with the following sentence: "Even my English, spoken with a Russian-French-German accent, is readily accepted by the children [urban ninth graders reading 3–4 years beneath grade level] who seem to have an amazing preference for insufficiency."

Conference and letter had a nearer relationship than coincidence in time, since a "preference for insufficiency" characterized children who were the subject of both. Just as a single, embattled teacher in New York was searching for help in educating the impoverished child (who happens, by remarkable coincidence, also to be the unsuccessful child), so had several dozen British and American teachers gathered for two weeks in the English Midlands to pursue that child's identity.

The following chapters speak of the impoverished child, of his abilities, his handicaps and advantages, his preferences and disinclinations. They also speak of his teachers and his community. In writing these chapters I have been guided by the belief that participants in any system of education which knowingly profits one group of children at another's expense, cannot expect to escape the despising of self which leads to moral despair.

1

O N E O F T H E M O S T interesting phrases used to describe some disadvantaged schoolchildren is "linguistically impoverished." Depending for its meaning more upon the person observing than the condition observed, the phrase encompasses children with various combinations of experiential, mental, and physical disabilities. In its wide range and inexact application, as well as in the damage it often does to those it apparently describes, it resembles more commonly misused words like neurotic, paranoid, and psychotic. Unlike those three terms, however, "linguistically impoverished" finds its chief victims amongst schoolchildren.

A minimal familiarity with symptoms of mania, schizophrenia, and paranoia is enough to convince anyone that most normal people exhibit occasional signs of all three diseases. When symptomatic, they may momentarily be manic, schizoid, or paranoid; nevertheless, no reasonable person would think them insane nor treat them as though they were mad.

In the same way, all of us who speak well show occasional symptoms of linguistic impoverishment. Who has not heard an eloquent speaker fumble for the right word, an elegant speaker mismatch verb and noun, or both inject several "uh's" and "you knows" into their sentences? Yet we are no more likely to believe these speakers impoverished than we are to believe the momentary paranoid insane. In both conditions, we recognize that characteristic symptoms require definition along dimensions both of frequency and degree.

Even these two dimensions, however, are not enough. A man who suffers recurring episodes of extreme elation and severe depression may be unsettled but sane; perhaps madness does not overtake him until he finds his depression unbearable and seeks to end his life. When suicidal tendencies have been added to a manic-depressive state—when symptoms appear in characteristic clusters—then a third necessary dimension has been added to frequency and degree.

Thus a child who speaks with limited vocabulary while reproducing sounds inaccurately may or may not be linguistically impoverished. But if the same child also speaks haltingly without physical defect and avoids situations which require words—then he exhibits a clustering of symptoms which points toward the disease of linguistic impoverishment.

Various symptoms which identify the disease fall generally into three categories. Most apparent of the three different types are the afflictions which beset the physical child. Sis was the most complete example of this kind of disability I have ever known. Before Cleo and Wentworth exposed him to the sound of himself on a tape recorder, before he began to believe himself worth something to others (and therefore worth something to himself), Sis incorporated into a single adolescent existence six characteristic physical symptoms of linguistic impoverishment. Perhaps the most important fact about all six as they appeared in Sis is that they were ameliorated by the remedy of attention, first to the impoverished ego which produced them and then to the symptoms themselves.

Sis invariably *spoke in a monotone.* All his coherent speech was as monotonic as his clothing was monochromatic, for he dressed his words in gray even as he clothed himself in his uncle's vast array of GI brown. Before he was adopted into the gang, his range of sound was extended only when he was angry; and when he was angry he was incoherent.

Even when Sis was angry, however, he was not fluent. Like so many other vastly inhibited children, he spoke unevenly no matter what his emotional condition. Fury varied his tone but it could not free his words. Sis *spoke haltingly without physical defect,* though his broken speech gave rise amongst his teachers to the myth of physical damage. Such myths are customary, and can be very convenient explanations of damage to children done by adults and then explained away by adults. Though customary and convenient, such explanations are seldom true.

A near and traditional companion to the myth of physical damage—"so many of *them* seem to have something *physically* wrong with them" a white teacher once told me, failing to place any emphasis at all upon "seem"—is the nonsense of inadequate hearing. The same teachers, school psychologists, and administrators who deduce brain damage from staggering speech patterns, also deduce subnormal hearing from sounds inaccurately reproduced. The truth is, I believe, that Sis and many thousands of children like him *reproduce sounds inaccurately* because they do not want to hear them, not because they cannot hear them.

The difference between *cannot* and *will not* is difficult to perceive and even more difficult to act upon. It is the difference, for instance, between teaching literacy and teaching the pleasures of literacy. Under pressure from the demanding attention of Cleo and Wentworth, taking double pleasure from their companionship and his own increasing proficiency, Sis proved whole of brain, palate, tongue, and ear. In spite of his reputation and appearance as a "damaged child"—which of course he was, though not in the way the description implied—he was able to attain reasonable fluency and accuracy in his speech. Before he could hear himself, he had to want to hear himself; before others could understand him, he had to care that they understood.

A child can speak monotonously and haltingly, as well as reproduce sounds inaccurately, and be at least partially understood. A stumbling monotone and a wide range of inaccuracy can be overcome by the listener's attention. When the listener's attention is distracted by physical peculiarities, however, then the contest becomes unequal and the battle for communication is lost. Such distractions are very commonly found in the physical habits of linguistically impoverished children.

Sis not only *looked away from his audience* when he spoke —invariably looked at some place other than where his intended auditor stood, and spoke toward that other place —but he always *partially blocked his mouth with his hand* and sometimes *exhibited signs of physical unease or discomfort*. In none of these practices was he unique within the gang, much less within the school. Only Cleo possessed none of the same habits. The other four were difficult to understand almost directly in proportion to the number of physical barriers they placed between themselves and their auditors.

Uncle Wiggly possessed fluent, multi-toned, accurate speech that was often nearly as difficult to comprehend as Sis's because of Uncle Wiggly's hyperactive motions. For the same reason, Rubbergut was easily understood so long as one did not look at him while he spoke. Otherwise, the various and unending movements of his remarkably flexible face combined with his constant readjustments of belt buckle and shirt buttons—nervous habits manifest only when he spoke—made his speech only partially intelligible.

During the early part of our acquaintance, before he felt fully comfortable with me, Wentworth spoke to me or to his friends in my presence from behind the barrier of his hand. Furthermore, he coughed so often when he spoke that I began to think he suffered from a bronchial disease. Several months passed before I realized that the cough, which could be spectacular, was partner to the interfering hand. Eventually I also came to understand that Wentworth had invented the cough to justify the constant presence of his hand in the vicinity of his mouth.

I do not mean to imply that Wentworth had consciously combined hand and cough into a protective device. What I am sure of is that he, like Sis, experiencing the distress of hearing and rejecting his own speech, was denying his responsibility for that speech with his characteristic cough and gesture. "Ain't me" Sis had said when he first heard himself on the tape recorder. "Ain't me" Wentworth was saying with all the nonverbal means at his command.

2

WHERE THE FIRST symptomatic category of the disease called "linguistic impoverishment" described the physical child, the second and third encompass symptoms sometimes less obvious because less intrusive. I chose to begin with physical manifestations because they are immediately more disturbing and consequently more liable to misinterpretation both by adults who confront them and children who possess them. In themselves, however, they are of minimal significance when compared with symptoms of failure in constructive and manipulative functions which beset the language and therefore afflict the lives of so many children.

By "constructive functions" of language I refer to those uses which primarily build meaning rather than manipulate environment. I am thinking, for example, of the difference between seldom using modifiers and seldom asking questions. Both modifiers and questions are linguistic in the broadest sense of the word, and absence of either can result in significant failures of communication. As I use the terms here, modifiers are constructive while questions are manipulative.

A practical instance of failure in constructive function is the example that arose out of contact between a hit-and-run truck and my rented car. On a Thursday when an early, light snow had briefly covered Washington at midday, a large truck sideslipped as it came up Tenth Street and struck the left front fender of my rented car. My evidence for the collision would have been limited to the crumpled fender had Snapper not witnessed the accident from a classroom window. He was very indignant when he came to see me:

" 'At mothah keep right on goin'!"

"Maybe he didn't know he hit it."

"He know. Slow up for a second, then stick his foot in 'er."

"Can you describe the truck?" My question was based on knowledge that two teachers had suffered similar damage to their cars during the autumn. One had observed and described a truck at a distance. Could the same driver be responsible?

"Sure," he answered happily. "It was a big one."

"How big?"

"Real big."

"Cab and trailer or all in one piece?"

"Man, I don't know...."

"What color was it?"

"Truck color."

Truck color. I wrote that one down. What do you do with a bright adolescent who wants to help, who has witnessed an event and can only describe its unmodified substance? Perhaps you do as I did—stop the questioning, thank him as sincerely as possible for his help, and ponder the nature of his testimony: Truck color. Real big. An average suburban child half Snapper's age would have done better than that.

To infer that the seven-year-old is therefore more intelligent than Snapper, is to infer nonsense. To infer that the child already has a richer visual experience than Snapper, is to infer a probable truth. Snapper's evidence, or lack of it, confronted me again with a phenomenon I first met in the language of boys in a Michigan reform school. For want of a better phrase, I have called it *habitually inadequate description*.

At first I attributed the lack of adjectives and adverbs in the boys' conversation to low intelligence; when I thought I knew better, I attributed it to inhibition. When I finally understood, I realized that I hadn't understood at all. Neither intelligence nor inhibition had anything to do with it. What had everything to do with it was habit which grew out of training so rigorous that it was reflected in every aspect of their language.

The training was both product of and protection against the terrible poverty of shape and color which afflicts lives confined within the tight boundaries of a few city blocks. Too much has been made of something called the "poverty of experience" of the urban poor, when the phrase really means "poor in experience like ours" and is far more an arbitrary judgment than a proven condition. A new translation is needed, one that assesses the objective fact of sense deprivation in urban ghetto life and relates barren language to barren environment rather than to intellectual or emotional inadequacies.

Nothing was wrong with Snapper's intellect or his powers of observation. Just as he was unprepared to meet a horse and a policeman on friendly terms, especially when the two were combined, so was he unprepared to note the details of a departing truck. Having spent years learning not to see his environment in order to preserve his humanity, he could not be expected to cure his selective blindness at a glance.

Far more important than the fact of his blindness, especially for those who teach and judge the Snappers of this world, is the fact of his selectivity. Neither as clever as Cleo nor as thoughtful as Wentworth, Snapper was the group's most acute observer of other human beings. Though only an adequate pool player, he was nevertheless a superb pool-room hustler because he never overestimated himself or underestimated his opponent. And after several hours in the poolroom, apparently concentrating on his own game or Sis's or mine, he would entertain us all with stories of who had been doing what to whom while we had been playing. As I listened to him during the spring of the year, and remembered that this was the same boy who had described the hit-and-run vehicle as "truck color," I came to know something more about the probable sources of linguistic impoverishment.

Closely associated with the habit of inadequate description is the practice of *using a very limited vocabulary*. I have purposefully italicized more than the customary *limited vocabulary* because I believe the significant impoverishment lies less often in the limits of possession than in the limits of usage. The idea that children who employ a narrow range of language necessarily do so because of intellectual restrictions is an idea that needs reassessment. In my experience, at least, many children habitually speak not only less well than they ought, but also less well than they can.

The same pressures in a different form that account for the selectivity of Snapper's vision, also produce the narrow working vocabulary of children like him. Snapper saw badly because he could not afford to see well; his environment offered no rewards for practicing the middle-class virtue of "being observant." Equally, children who have relatively broad vocabularies at their potential command—words whose meaning they know and whose application they understand—are often dissuaded from using them by their environment.

Negative pressures which restrict the working vocabulary of so many children come primarily from two separate sources. Least recognized of the two is disapproval of influential adults, especially those of the immediate family. The well-reported romance of first-generation American children who learned and spoke English words that both baffled and delighted their immigrant parents, is a tale without parallel in many of today's ghetto families. Bafflement is now far more likely to lead to anger and retaliation than to delight and reward. It was Cleo who revealed the change to me.

We were returning from District News Company and the memorable reception given us by Joe Ottenstein. That anybody—especially someone they had actually met—should have enough money to be able to give it away, was occupying my companions' entire attention. Everything about the act of regularly giving money away, even the name for it, fascinated them:

"How you say that word?"

"Phil-an-thro-py."

"Pretty fancy word."

"Nothing's too fancy for giving money away." Cleo had interrupted the conversation between Snapper and me. For the first time I was aware of her alternate dialect—she had spoken the last syllable of "Nothing's" and "giving" like a teacher of elocution—but my next comment brought such an unexpected response that I had no time to think about anything else.

"I use the word all the time," I said. "I want to be ready in case I ever have the money."

"All right for you." Cleo's voice was noncommittal.

"You're not figuring to have any loose money?"

"Naw. Not figurin' on usin' that word."

"What's wrong with it?" I had heard her as she picked up the dialect again.

"My momma don't wanna hear it in my mouth."

"Your mother doesn't. . . ." I was astounded. What in the world was wrong with "philanthropy"? "What's wrong with it? Does she know what it means?"

"Naw. That what's wrong with it."

And that was very wrong indeed, as I discovered in many different ways during the course of the year. Though Cleo had experienced the worst case of negative influence from her family—her mother was tough, smart, almost illiterate, and full of resentment at her own ignorance—she exemplified an affliction as common in her gang as it was amongst her peers. Of the four boys, only Uncle Wiggly did not suffer from some degree of pressure to speak as the adults in his family spoke. At his mother's request he shared with her the best of his school reading materials; she was quick to praise his expanding vocabulary and to try some of the words herself.

In contrast to the positive support of Uncle Wiggly's mother, was the negative influence of Wentworth's peers in his dumbhead English class. Their pressure for conformation represents the second source of infection for the ghetto epidemic of artificially impoverished language:

Parents, like teachers, can often be handled; if not neutralized, their power can be diminished by minimal contact, which was Cleo's most effective defense against her mother. Few children living in severely restricted physical space like Wentworth's school and neighborhood, manage to limit their peer contacts and keep their mental health. Even the Wentworth who had resolved to "do it different" could not afford to antagonize his peers. Instead, he chose to protect himself with the armor of manifest stupidity— even when he began to read openly—in most of his classroom encounters.

A striking example of this kind of political impoverishment was acted out in front of me one Friday afternoon in

Wentworth's English class. Perhaps because it was Friday afternoon, with the week almost finished and the week's lesson plans completed, the dumbhead English teacher— normally a martinet with no apparent sense that pleasure (for the children) had anything to do with teaching—was indulging her class. Several boys were carrying copies of *Hot Rod* magazine. Beginning. there, the discussion progressed to some of the more technical aspects of hot-rodding:

"Gonna get me a '53 Ford and chop 'er." One of Wentworth's classmates, declaring his intentions when he was old enough to put together a license and a little capital.

"How about a bull-nose?" The teacher's question was so unexpected from her that peripheral conversations stopped abruptly.

"What you know about bull-nosing?" asked the boy, suspiciously, who planned to chop a Ford.

"Plenty," she said and smiled broadly, enjoying the sensation her words were causing in the class. "My son chopped and bull-nosed cars before you knew what a hot-rod was. Plenty of things I know I don't go around telling everybody. Do you know what it means to *french* a car?"

Her question challenged the boy who had wanted to hear her on the subject of bull-nosing. When he had to admit that he didn't know, the teacher turned her question to the class:

"Does anyone know what *frenching* is?" It was an unfortunate question, with its unintended sexual allusion bringing the class to the verge of hysteria. But the teacher recovered nicely—"All right, all right. I know about *that*, too. But which of you knows what it means to french a car?"

Apparently no one did. But two people in that class knew its ignorance was more apparent than real, because Wentworth and I both knew how to french a car. I knew that he knew because he had once referred to the process and explained it to all of us during an afternoon's conversation. I stared at him in consternation and amazement as his face mirrored the blank expressions of his classmates.

I put it to him that afternoon. Why had he denied his knowledge when everybody would have welcomed the answer?

"Not ever'body," he responded softly.

"Who?" I asked. "The teacher wanted to hear it from somebody. . . ."

"Naw," he said, "not her. Ole Billy."

"Billy? The boy up front who was talking about bull-nosing?"

"Yeah. One who didn't know nothin' about frenchin'."

Slowly, he made me understand. Wentworth had no intention of making Billy look or feel any worse in front of the class. Far preferable to that was to keep quiet, to keep his knowledge to himself, to let the teacher think him and the class as ignorant as they appeared. After all, what more could be lost by dumbheads if a teacher obtained one more proof of their incompetence? But Billy, and whoever showed him up, had something more valuable to protect than doubted intellect. They had their place in the group to conserve.

Just as environmental requirements can artificially restrict children's working vocabulary, similar requirements can have equally powerful effects upon other constructive functions of language. One of the most familiar observations about speech patterns of impoverished children is that they tend toward use of a single tense, the present. A common explanation for this restricted usage is the undeveloped ear of the child together with the negative reinforcement of his language community:

"Where did he throw the ball, John?"

"He throw it into the bushes."

"No, he *threw* it into the bushes."

"What I say—he throw it into the bushes."

Which is what he said; he just didn't say it right. Both underdeveloped ear and negative reinforcement of the community—which may often be effect and cause—are credible explanations; though credible and even necessary, these explanations are insufficient to account for *habitual use of the present tense.*

In order to arrive at a more satisfactory explanation of the dominant present tense, as well as to understand other conditions which are said to characterize the mental life of linguistically impoverished children, we must look beyond the capacities of children and toward the incapacitating restrictions of their environment. Many observers have commented on a *preoccupation with things* that dominates the content of some disadvantaged children's speech in the same proportion that the present tense dominates its form. Responsibility for this imbalance is usually assigned to environmental deprivation, the assumption being that absence of things and ideas leads to desire for the former and unfamiliarity with the latter.

The assumption, I believe, is only symptomatically correct, i.e., it describes the discomfort but not the disease. Unfortunately, diagnosticians have so thoroughly confused the two that they have mistaken palliatives for remedies; the best that can be said of their efforts at treatment is that their patients often die in comfort.

In place of the convenient discomfort of an environment without material or conceptual riches—convenient because the remedy seems encompassable in a wealthy, educated society—I believe we must recognize a disease far less easy to cure. Habitual use of the present tense and a preoccupation with things may both be blamed upon environmental deprivation, but neither submits to the cure of enrichment.

Though these symptoms of linguistic impoverishment may be repressed by increased contact with things and ideas, the disease which causes them soon becomes embedded in belief rather than experience and cannot be removed by knowledge alone.

When the past is consistently unhappy and the future unlikely to be different, the present becomes all of time that is bearable. When ideas and concepts have no demonstrable affective value—when the world remains immovable no matter your lever or footing—then things may become both haven and support. In order to protect themselves from the damage of past remembered and future feared, from the humiliation of a world summarily immune to their intellectual influence, children learn to limit their aspirations as well as their vocabularies. The natural and inevitable effect of truncated hope is a world defined by the immediate and the tangible.

Understanding the malaise of spirit which produces widespread failure in constructive functions of language also leads to a clear view of another condition apparently endemic in linguistically impoverished children. One of the most popular insights into the mentality of such children is that they are not very good at working with abstractions. When examined carefully, this observation seems to be composed of two different assessments: Disadvantaged children are even more uncomfortable than other children with abstract reality; and they seem to have less than average ability to store certain kinds of information. According to one of my sources, a female junior high school teacher, "they have terrible memories and they don't understand anything they can't touch."

This teacher was speaking of Appalachian white immigrants in a Detroit inner-city school. But she might just as well have been describing Cleo, Wentworth, and all their friends as they were seen by many of their teachers at Garnet-Patterson Junior High School in Washington, D.C. Such observations are not only independent of race and location, they are too often independent of children as well and have far more to do with the observer's imperception than the children's inability.

When viewed from the vantage point of a life where time is a positive dimension and concepts are good currency, the memory and abstract understanding of impoverished children must appear inferior by comparison. The appearance, I believe, is deceiving, and is largely the result of a false assumption by the beholder. That assumption is the belief that both memory and abstract understanding are abilities significantly independent of attitudes, that only extreme emotional states are likely to have any noticeable effect upon these basic human capacities.

Though such an assumption is comforting to adults who believe that performance is essentially independent of motivation (count a remarkably high proportion of teachers in that group), it is an assumption which damages children out of all proportion to the meager comfort it brings to adults. Consider the case of Eddie, Wentworth's classmate and sometime friend:

We were talking about baseball. I was going to Baltimore for the weekend to visit my family and to attend a baseball game.

"You know a lot about baseball?" Wentworth asked. I had just answered Snapper's question about Baltimore's chances of winning the pennant and my answer gave more information than the question required.

"Yes. I like to read the sports pages."

"You play?"

"Once I did. But not any more."

"Who the last guy hit four hunnert?"

"Ted Williams."

"Yeah. Who the onliest pitcher win mor'n a hunnert games in both leagues?"

I had no idea and said so. Had he been reading the record book just to be able to put me down?

"Aw naw man. Wouldn't do that. Don't have to, anyways. Just ask Eddie. He know it all."

And so I met Eddie, who possessed the most nearly encyclopedic baseball knowledge of any person I have ever known. Only books have more information, but not much more. Even to a man raised with boys who prided themselves on knowing the full roster of every major league team and the performance history of every man on every roster —plus most of the exotic facts that compose the statistical history of baseball—even to me Eddie was astounding.

"Tell him all the people in 'at Hall, Eddie. Go on. Tell him."

All the people in that Hall were all the members of the Baseball Hall of Fame in Cooperstown, New York. Eddie not only knew their names, he knew everything written about their baseball lives and all he could discover about their personal histories. So much information so completely available to the memory of any human being would be cause for admiration, no matter what the subject. But that the information should be in Eddie's possession would have been a staggering revelation to some of his teachers, for he was classified by them as "retarded."

The undeniable fact is that Eddie was "retarded" if school performance was the measuring stick of his intellect. Physically small and temperamentally mild, he had a shrunken presence which caused his teachers to stop for a moment's thought when his name was mentioned: Oh, yes, Eddie . . . well, not much I can tell you. Nice boy, but a little simple. Had to think for a minute when you mentioned his name because he doesn't make a strong impression. Don't know much about him, I'm afraid. He doesn't bother me so I don't bother him. Ha ha. Older than the rest—going to be sixteen soon, I think, and that'll be the end of school for him. Just as well, probably. Doesn't seem to be all there, if you know what I mean.

Yes, I knew what he meant. The same boy who could select and remember most of the significant figures from one reading of a pageful of baseball statistics; who could do the mental arithmetic of batting averages to three decimal places, given times-at-bat and number of hits; who could recite interminable lists of names complete not only with middle names but nicknames as well—this was also the boy who appeared to have almost no information to bring to bear upon the problems of classroom learning. To put it another way, he didn't seem to be able to remember anything useful.

For Eddie, as for so many others, what was useful and what was learned in school were utterly unrelated. Eddie not only knew baseball, he knew automobiles as well. He could supply year and maker for any postwar American car and for many foreign cars that passed through his neighborhood. He knew nothing of their mechanical nature and cared nothing for it. His care and comfort was his knowledge; that it described real men and automobiles was almost irrelevant for him. *Knowing* was reason enough for knowing, and he bent himself to the task with an undistracted attention.

That Eddie could devote himself with such single-mindedness to baseball and cars was a powerful tribute to his concentration and a devastating condemnation of his school. In spite of the beliefs of his teachers, his retardation was entirely elective. Also in spite of their beliefs, memory is often significantly dependent upon motivation. The unmoved child is the unable child, "a little simple" in the unperceiving eyes of those who do not or will not understand that even the simplest organism withdraws from the experience of pain.

The principle of usefulness applies equally to abstract learning. Children who "don't understand anything they can't touch" are not necessarily children who *can't* understand. The equivalence is as easy as it is irresponsible, taking only the apparent evidence of the child's performance as its criterion for judgment. New evidence must be sought, this time in the area of the child's feelings about intangible things.

A striking example of negative feelings in children which directly affected their capacity for abstract thought was related to me by a clergyman who spent one day each week with boys in an Illinois reform school. While describing our work in Michigan to the school's faculty and staff, I had emphasized our conclusions about the substantial difference between real and apparent intellect in many impoverished children. When my speech was done and the subsequent discussion completed, I heard this brief story from a man who told it as the worst experience of his ministerial life:

An English teacher had been using C. S. Lewis's science fiction trilogy with a group of his brightest students. The teacher had used the three books before with some success in the tenth grade of a public school and saw no reason why they wouldn't meet with greater success in reform school, where he thought his best students to be more able than their public school counterparts. More able they may have been, but the trilogy was only half the success with them that it had been with the other children.

The equal half was the literal half. Two of Lewis's three books deal with adventures upon Mars and Venus, adventures which the reform school boys compared favorably with other space-and-time stories by Robert Heinlein, Ray Bradbury, and Isaac Asimov. But the teacher's purpose in using the books had not been solely to compare them with other science fiction the boys had read. He had also intended them to be a bridge between literal and allegorical literature, an introduction to several of the livelier books of the Old Testament. In fulfilling that intent, they failed completely.

Part of Lewis's theme is the confrontation between good and evil and the nature of temptation in a Christian context. Experiencing no success in bringing the allegory to his students' attention, the teacher turned to the most appropriate available resource for help. Enter the Christian minister, full—as he himself said—"of good intentions and pure ignorance."

His intentions were to explicate Lewis's allegory and to translate impersonal, abstract ideas of good, evil, and divinity into personal, concrete experience which would draw the boys beyond the books and into themselves. His ignorance was his belief that he could translate all three abstractions with equal vigor. What had been an intellectual defeat for the teacher became an emotional humiliation for the minister as he discovered his inability to engage the boys in meaningful discussion of an abstract idea called divinity.

Good and evil meant a lot to them, he told me. One of their favorite ways of looking at the difference was to draw the fine lines between actions of their friends "outside" and actions that had gotten them into reform school. It was no great leap from that distinction, he said, to speaking about relative good and evil; the warmth of the discussion had prompted him to go on to Lewis's idea of God.

Go on he did, to absolutely no effect. "They wouldn't talk about their God or anybody's God," he said. "At first I thought they would if I could provoke them to it. Then I

thought they simply weren't up to it. Finally I realized that
they just *wouldn't*. Not couldn't. Not even wouldn't because
they actively didn't want to. Just wouldn't because the whole
idea of divinity seemed to be *useless* to them. And I was
never able to make it useful."

Teachers and psychologists as well as ministers have
frequently observed that one symptom of intellectual inadequacy is difficulty in dealing with abstract ideas. Few have
been as perceptive as that reform school clergyman who
made the difference between disability and disinclination in
impoverished children. Just as he could not infuse the notion
of God with usefulness for children who had seen no evidence of a divine presence in their own blighted lives, so
have we who teach and judge the same children been unable
to convince them of the use of so many concepts (like
justice) which inform our world. True to ourselves, as
always, we have cast doubts upon their intellect rather than
upon our persuasiveness or our values.

3

THE THIRD CATEGORY of symptoms which may identify the disease of linguistic impoverishment includes those surface eruptions and deeper weaknesses afflicting the manipulative functions of language. A child who *seldom asks questions* may be so rich in answers that he finds questions unnecessary; or he may understand so little that he cannot formulate a sensible query; or he may be afraid of the dialogue which the question-and-answer process implies. By itself, the absence of questions is an inscrutable symptom, offering little in the way of useful evidence for the child's linguistic condition.

The absence of questions, however, is not usually a singular symptom when found in linguistically impoverished children. Very often, perhaps even always and certainly in a great number of cases, the impoverished child who seldom asks questions is the child who *seldom explains*. The customary jargon for describing this condition states that "cause and effect relationships are lacking" in the child's speech. With or without jargon, the relationship between failure to ask questions and failure to explain is as near as the relationship between linguistic impoverishment and failure in school.

One striking and significant difference between classrooms full of promising and unpromising children is the identity of the verbal discourse: Unpromising children make comments that invite no response; promising children make comments that are often questions and almost always invitations to a dialogue. Clearly the former are as unable to manipulate their classroom environment as the latter are unable to refrain from that manipulation. Sadly, inevitably, it is the manipulative children who most easily gain attention and affection from their teachers.

Ability to meet the vocal needs and requirements of teachers who are like and unlike themselves (linguistically rich and poor children, respectively) is too often the keystone upon which success and failure in the schools is built. Large numbers of teachers have told me of children who "seem to welcome failure," the comment often being made with equal measure of chagrin and surprise. The chagrin appears to me fully warranted, but not the surprise. Linguistically impoverished children are poor in speech and its attendant habits; there is nothing necessarily wrong with their intellects. They know perfectly well that a likely consequence of their vocal passivity is failure.

The nature of vocal passivity may best be understood when viewed against the background of *verbal* and *vocal* as basic linguistic distinctions, distinctions which are of great importance to teachers and pupils alike. Verbality and vocality, as descriptions, are relatively simple. The verbal child is one who translates his thoughts into unspoken words; the vocal child habitually adds the dimension of spoken language to the words which clothe his thoughts. The latter child is not necessarily more able than the former, but he is certainly more amenable to classroom education as classrooms are presently organized and conducted.

Teachers of advantaged children, at whatever level, are familiar with students who cannot bring themselves to participate actively in classroom discussions but who perform remarkably well in written work. As I wrote "students who cannot bring themselves" I saw female images of girls and women I have taught who covered themselves with silence in class discussion and with glory in written assignments. Their sex may be relevant to their performance in this way:

Classroom discussion tends to be conducted under the same rules and assumptions that govern games with balls usually played by boys. Rapid intervention and extraction, visible responsiveness, and apparent aggressiveness, reactions which are at a premium in such games, are equally useful in classroom discussions. Perhaps for the same reason that girls seldom play these games, as well as because they seldom play these games (a different thing), I should have written that we who teach advantaged children are familiar with the child who cannot bring *herself* to participate actively in classroom discussions. This familiarity should prepare us to consider the vital differences between verbal and vocal disadvantage, and the implications of those differences for teaching children who seem not only to expect but to invite failure.

Just as some highly verbal female students are handicapped in the vocal interaction of the classroom, so are some verbal children handicapped by the highly vocal expectations of their teachers. This difference between verbality and vocality may be a sexual difference of no great importance in educating the advantaged, but it may be a cultural difference of all importance in educating the disadvantaged whose impoverishment often takes the form of speaking in a monotone, using a very limited vocabulary, reproducing sounds inaccurately, seldom asking questions or explaining anything, and rarely engaging in dialogue with adults.

The force of observing these characteristics must be

toward convincing any teacher responsible for educating such children that the demands of vocality are those which they are least likely to meet. Furthermore, this conviction may lead teachers to discover that classroom demands for vocality are more a function of the teacher's personality and preparation than of the child's need.

Teachers are customarily of a social class and human kind which places great faith in the spoken word. Since everything in their experience as students and teachers tends to support that faith—e.g., when they were students, they were good students because they spoke up; when they were student-teachers, their instructors filled them full of vocal methods and vocal discriminations; when they became teachers, they learned to recognize their good students primarily by the quality of their vocal response—they translate their faith into a self-fulfilling prophesy in the classroom: He who speaks well thinks well; he who speaks badly thinks badly; therefore, he who does not speak does not think. And thus most of the sad children who lack vocality, for whatever reason, but who may possess both words and thoughts, come to know themselves (even as they are known) as the educationally unfit of our time.

The child who seldom asks questions and even more rarely explains himself is often the abnormally quiet child who is noisy at the wrong time. In fact, *inability to discriminate between noisy and quiet responses* is a third characteristic symptom of manipulative failure in the linguistically impoverished child. Coupled with *too-ready agreement*, poor selection of appropriate response is probably the single heaviest classroom burden of the unpromising child.

If not for all such children, then at least it was an unbearable weight for Uncle Wiggly's narrow shoulders. The same Uncle Wiggly whose mother shared his schoolbooks with him, who spoke well if rarely, who navigated with confidence and accuracy—this same adolescent was so unreliable in his classroom responses that he would have been a legend in his own time in a suburban junior high school. At Garnet-Patterson he was considered only mildly remarkable.

If Uncle Wiggly was extraordinary, it was only as an exaggeration of his classmates and peers. Where most of them often agreed with whatever Authority said, sometimes no matter how absurd the statement, Uncle Wiggly *always* agreed. His overwhelming acquiescence was like that of most children who are just learning to speak. Often understanding nothing except the tone of what is said to them, they will agree to anything if the tone of the speaker seems to ask for agreement. Pliable as they are, they are no more malleable than Uncle Wiggly in the classroom.

A myth for our time based upon several books and motion pictures has grown about the classroom responses and school actions of poor children. The myth has so much apparent substance today that the recruitment of teachers to work in inner-city schools has been bent out of shape by its weight. Many teachers of teachers find their students convinced that inner-city schools are full of surly, nasty children whose chief entertainment is teacher-baiting and chief joy is violence. These expectations corrupt the motivation not only of teachers who refuse to face such problems but also of those who choose to do so, for both too often base their actions on a view that is utterly false.

The practice of really unpleasant teacher-baiting by nasty children is far more prevalent in suburban than urban schools. Judging from my own experiences and that of my former students who have taught in both places, the very frequent vocal violence of some privileged children is far more to be feared than the very infrequent physical violence of their disadvantaged counterparts. What is most to be feared by all those teachers who are concerned for the survival of impoverished children is the terrible acquiescence, with its subsequent inappropriate responses, that marks and mars their classroom life.

Uncle Wiggly was subject to that acquiescent action which produces in its victims the reaction of unpredictable noise and silence. Though he wiggled constantly in class as if the temperature of his seat were rising beneath him, he came to a boil only occasionally and then at no constant heat. Neither his teachers nor I ever had the slightest clue as to what determined his selection of individual responses in the classroom, though I came to be certain by the end of the year that what we saw in him was the release of equal and opposite forces built up by his initial, abject acquiescence.

Both like and unlike the agreeable infant, Uncle Wiggly apparently agreed with Authority so often not because his primary motive was to please but because he was insufficiently in command of his language to do otherwise. Often he made it clear, in other contexts, that he did not believe in the words and actions of his classroom self, and that he bitterly resented both the teachers' questions and his own responses that combined to make him look and feel like a fool. Perhaps that resentment was the basic and sufficient reason for his inveterate *distrust of vocal people* and his *minimal conversation with adults*.

These two symptoms of disease in the manipulative functions of language are especially characteristic of linguistic impoverishment. Except for Rubbergut, who included adults and vocal people within the broad sweep of his affection, Uncle Wiggly shared both symptoms in almost equal virulence with his friends. The two were closely related in all the children, for it was the adults in their lives—especially school adults—who talked the most. I believe, however, that this distrust of adults is at least as much a distrust of self by the children who manifest it as it is a distrust of the adults to whom it is apparently directed.

In spite of my expectations, the most formidable barrier between members of Cleo's gang and me was built neither of age, color, nor affluence. It was, instead, constructed of my language and their distrust of all extensive conversation. This was especially true early in our relationship where my conversation tended too often toward explanation and their reaction tended toward outrage derived from suspicions of being patronized. The truth is that I was patronizing them, as almost all teacherly adults tend to do, and their reaction was partially justified. Perhaps the most interesting aspect of this confrontation was that they learned to tolerate and forgive me long before I learned to modify my behavior toward them.

One memorable example of the children's distrust of very vocal people came in a brief moment during our farewell party at Mack's apartment. Wentworth had discovered in his jacket the piece of paper from our visit to the University of Maryland which had Rob's name, address, and campus telephone written upon it. Cleo had seen me handling it, had asked what it was, and dismissed Rob with one of her very few final condemnations: "That boy," she said, turning away with an offended expression on her face, "he talk too much."

4

CHILDREN WHO CAN fairly be described as linguistically impoverished tend also to exhibit certain characteristic personal habits which, though nonlinguistic, have considerable effect upon their language and their learning. These traits divide themselves into two groups, one formed by the child's view of his world and the other based upon his view of himself. Though each group has its own identity, they are interdependent signs of malnourished, naked children whose instincts for survival turn them back into themselves for sustenance and protection.

Transparence, invisibility, disappearance—all forms of self-protection and all employed by children who have learned that their absence is more desired than their presence. They are the *self-effacing* ones; even the best of them, like Eddie, learn to bury themselves beneath a mountain of mildness and baseball statistics. Their retreat can range from a relatively innocuous disembodied classroom presence to an exceptionally dangerous tolerance for pain. This latter characteristic is the logical extension of a life without complaint. Especially by comparison with their more advantaged peers, impoverished children *seldom complain.* Even in schools with a very wide range of privilege and poverty, more fortunate children are likely to be more frequent complainers. I do not mean to identify advantage with complaint; rather, I believe privileged children learn early that just complaints are likely to receive fair attention. Impoverished children, learning equally early that no complaint is likely to provoke positive response, learn not to complain.

The self-effacing refusal to complain can be a virtue or a self-destructive vice. While visiting a Detroit high school I heard the story of a boy who had gone through an entire school day with a badly broken leg because he "hadn't wanted to make no trouble." The gym teacher who had driven him to the hospital had seen the boy knocked down on the school's outdoor basketball court before classes began, had seen him get up with difficulty and refuse to continue playing, and then had seen him again six hours later in the boys' locker room as he dressed for his last period gym class. The teacher had felt sick to his stomach, he said, when he saw the boy's leg.

The boy who doesn't want to make trouble about his leg —suppose it's not broken, suppose it just hurts?—may also be the boy who *takes little pride in his own work* and is as *suspicious of praise* as he is *indifferent to criticism.* When a child views himself as insufficient, when his pride has suffered the diminishment of unrelieved failure, then he learns to protect the little pride that remains to him by hoarding it and hiding it from his enemies. As his sense of his own inadequacy is confirmed into certainty, he becomes naturally suspicious of all praise and begins to place himself beyond the reach of criticism.

This prideless, suspicious, indifferent child can be found to exist in the same form both within and beyond the boundaries of the classroom. Though he exists in the same form in both school and community, the degree of his afflictions is often so exacerbated by the school environment that he sometimes seems to be a creature different in kind when he inhabits the classroom. This change is never more marked or more damaging than when it affects the quality of the child's imagination.

The child who *functions badly in activities of the imagination* in school may be so changed outside the confines of the classroom that he is all but unrecognizable by contrast. During my year of close association with Cleo and her boys, I came to know a good many of their friends in the school. Though I knew none of them well, I came to be known to them as Cleo and Wentworth's friend and therefore less to be feared or avoided than the usual school adult. By spring, and occasionally before, my presence was often taken for granted and did not alter or interrupt their activities.

The most valuable privilege that acceptance gained for me was the opportunity to see all the children living as a group within the natural habitat created by their own imaginations. Months before, having noted the withdrawal of less able ones in the face of classroom demands upon their imagination, I had explained their withdrawal to myself in convenient terms of inadequate experience and limited intellect. The terms were as wrong as they were convenient. What I was seeing was the protective camouflage of children who have learned that participation in the classroom, unsafe in every way, is most to be avoided when the invitation begins with the word, "Suppose. . . ."

Because a free imagination seems so much a part of childhood to adults who never knew the need to hobble their own imaginations when they were children, those adults who are teachers are surprised and frustrated by the refusal of so many impoverished children to rise to the bait of "Suppose. . . ." The experience is very widespread, for I have seen it myself in the United States and England and had it described to me by former students and colleagues teaching in almost every corner of American poverty. Their experiences and mine are remarkably alike in discovering children who habitually fail, from choice rather than from necessity, to participate in classroom activities of the imagination.

My first clear view of the effect of linguistic impoverishment on the ready imagination of children came through the paired magnifying glasses of Wentworth's and Cleo's dumbhead and smarthead classes. Since both children were in the ninth grade, their classes—in company with the other ninth grades—spent certain periods of time together during the day. Whether at lunch or recess or gym, whether before or after school so long as they were outside of the classroom, the two classes were not easily separable by the *quantity* of their imaginative play.

As with any other children, no matter their economic or social condition, the quick ones and the slow ones identified themselves by the varying *quality* of their imaginative play. But likenesses were more striking than differences—dumbhead and smarthead children were not so separate in their mode of imaginative play as their performance in the classroom seemed to promise. Children who reacted with passivity, truculence, or downright anger when invited to use their imaginations in class, were competent and even eager participants in imaginative games played with their peers outside of class.

The self-effacing, uncomplaining, apparently unimaginative and indifferent child is also likely to be found at the center of a schoolroom paradox defined by the contradiction between his wants and his needs. The tensions produced by this paradox are reflected in the extraordinary *upset from broken routine* which marks his reaction to varied schedules and activities, and his almost *desperate hold upon the familiar*. These two closely related characteristics have both been serious problems for adults who would alter the education of the linguistically impoverished child.

When the program called "English In Every Classroom" was first introduced into Maxey Boys Training School and, again, when it was translated into Garnet-Patterson Junior High School, the original classroom and library reactions of students in both schools were so similar that we felt justified in describing generalized patterns on the basis of relatively small samples. As striking as the similarity was between school-wide reactions, it was no more powerful than the dissimilarity between classroom and library acceptance inside both institutions.

Original classroom reactions by better students in both schools ranged from passive acceptance to great enthusiasm; generally, however, the less competent the student the worse the reaction. We were amazed (and a little outraged) when the worst students in Maxey became the worst enemies of the program as it was manifest in the classroom. "These ain't no kinda textbooks," we were told again and again as we passed out newspapers, magazines, and paperbound books. "How we gonna learn anythin' from these? Don't nobody use these in *regular* school!"

When we recovered from self-righteous disappointment, we realized how poignant the contrast was between the words and the boys who spoke them. Almost invariably we were hearing complaints from those with the most consistent records of academic failure and least likelihood of returning successfully to "regular" school. We soon understood that they were gripped by their all-encompassing fear of change, that their reaction was not to the materials themselves but to the fact of change. Our evidence for the source of their anguish was the contrast between their initial rejection of new materials in the classroom and their immediate acceptance of those same materials in the library.

In both schools, children who balked at using ephemeral materials for textbooks did not hesitate to accept drugstore spinners full of paperback books and tables heaped with every popular magazine as substitutes for the customary shelves of hardbound books. At least one reason for this differential acceptance was the unfamiliarity of students at both institutions with libraries of any description. Since no library configuration could possibly challenge their combined senses of propriety and custom, they were immediately comfortable in a reading room that resembled no other.

Those of us who were engaged in the experiment at Maxey School are unlikely to forget a boy's dour comment that we savoured and repeated for several years as a kind of last word from our difficult clientele. The boy's English teacher had found him in the library reading J. H. Griffin's *Black Like Me*, the same book he had actually refused to accept from her as a textbook when she had distributed paperback copies to his class earlier in the week. When she was unable to refrain from pointing out that he was reading a library copy of exactly the book he had refused in class, he looked up only long enough to dismiss her and her accusation with a single comment: "Ain't tryin' to learn nothin' here."

5

A REASONABLY MALLEABLE child would not have been as difficult (or perhaps as interesting) as that intransigent young man. For malleable children—those who take the imprint of their teachers' own education—are the joy of our schools. Because their environment reinforces the values implicit in their instruction, they can be taught as though they were miniatures of those who bear them, teach them and employ them. Ductile, docile, and determined to succeed, they will perform in school because the air they breathe carries the virus of the school-performance message: perform now, profit later.

They, their parents, and their children play no part in the adversary culture which characterizes the relationship between many urban schools and people they are supposed to serve. Though suburban schools customarily live in concert with their clientele, urban schools often find themselves in utter disharmony with their communities. Teachers and parents of impoverished children are traditional adversaries, frozen in a confrontation which has much to do with the problem of teaching literacy in the schools.

Someone has said that half the college graduates in the United States never read another book after leaving school. The accuracy of the fraction is unimportant, not only because it is thoroughly believable, but also because the immense sale of magazines and newspapers to college graduates is enough evidence that they regard literacy as a lever to move the mass of necessity, if not as a key to open the door of pleasure. We may grieve for their sensibility, but we need not worry about their survival. They have, after all, learned their lesson well. They were taught that reading is a means to the end of obtaining right answers. In their lengthy school careers, pleasure was as irrelevant to reading as it was to learning. Having read sufficiently to obtain their degrees, they can hardly be expected to initiate a practice (reading for pleasure) which is alien to their preparation.

Let us suppose, however, that we are dealing with children who are not so adept as their middle-class counterparts at postponing the relationship between cause and effect. These are children who need to see immediate returns from each investment because they do not learn gratification deferment as one of the immutable facts of their communal life. These are also children who learn to expect and even to welcome failure because they live in a world hostile to the shape of school-taught literacy and because they learn not to care about obtaining right answers in school. Let us further suppose that a child who is not successful at obtaining right answers through reading, and who does not learn that reading can serve the purpose of pleasure, is likely to learn that reading is good for nothing except the pain of recurrent failure. Even an impoverished child learns to avoid pain if he can.

Avoidance of pain is also the child's likeliest reaction to being caught between the adversary values of home and school. When the eighteen-word sentences of his classroom

clash with the eight-word sentences of his family and neighborhood, he is virtually certain to avoid the pain of difference, suspicion, and derogation by avoiding his new
literacy. Like a muscle unused, it weakens and atrophies
until it is useless to its possessor. Or it perishes so rapidly
that it can never be said to have grown at all.

These suppositions lead to two separate hypotheses.
Neither is sufficient to account for the relationship between
impoverishment and failure in school, though both are
necessary to comprehend its significance. First, it is possible
that reading may be made repugnant to school-oriented
children without doing them severe damage, but conse-
quences are likely to be far more serious for children not
oriented toward school. Second, it seems entirely probable
that literacy may not satisfactorily be taught in school to
children caught between opposing forces of an adversary
culture.

The first hypothesis, both more common and more
acceptable because less extreme, bears a burden of ines-
capable proof. Where is the educator who claims that children "not going on to college" (an awkward phrase for an
awkward situation) are learning a useful literacy? Novel
school programs for teaching such children continue to pro-
liferate; unless patently foolish, they are readily accepted
by teachers they most seriously affect. Inventors of such
programs are surprised again and again by the warm welcome teachers give to their inventions. But who, after all, is
likely to know more about damage being done to anti-
literate children by traditional methods and materials?

This damage is not conjectural; it is specific, and clearly
visible. Some of its manifestations are the typical reticence
and violence which characterize the vocal and physical communication of anti-literate children. The child who learns to
distrust language is the child who leaves it in disuse while he

retreats into a world that accepts physical communication. He becomes the adolescent and adult who must rely upon the available violence of action to replace the unavailable force of language. In so doing, he becomes—even in his own eyes—a kind of social leper.

His illness, however, may be curable when radical remedies are employed. At least two diseased portions of his schoolroom experience can be identified and subjected to remediation. First of these is his English teacher, a creature sick to death from the loneliness which isolates his reason for being from the context which justifies his existence. English teachers exist to teach English. If they are fortunate, they perceive the glory of their subject; if they are extraordinary, they communicate its beauty to their students. But no matter what their quality, teaching at least a functional literacy is the basic justification of their vocational existence. Consider the impossibility of their task with linguistically impoverished children:

Such children, sometimes called "terminal" students (a word borrowed from the language of death by teachers who recognize their true vocations) are also identified by their teachers as "practical" children. This use of the word seems intended to identify children who are uncomfortable when working with abstractions and unhappy when asked to imagine the relationship between a cause and the distant effect it is meant to produce. What this means for the English class is that practical students want a clear statement of the return on their potential investment before they suffer the pains of raising the necessary capital. What this means for the English teachers' characteristic isolation is that it is often an insuperable barrier between practical children and literacy. If only English teachers teach English, if only English teachers care very much about reading and writing, then practical children soon learn that reading and writing can safely be ignored. And of course they are ignored by the multitude of practical children who learn only what they have to.

If this analysis is correct, then one effective change in the relationship between isolated English teachers and practical children would be to make an English teacher of every teacher in every classroom. Its purpose is to prevent the practical child from opting out, to prevent growth of his suspicion that English is the concern only of English teachers. Because practical children are not necessarily foolish children, they usually learn what they must in order to survive. When each teacher in each classroom *demands reading and writing each day*, a remarkable event occurs: Practical children learn how to read and write. They learn because, practically speaking, they cannot do otherwise.

The second diseased portion of the classroom experience that causes the sickness of anti-literacy is the text which the practical child is directed to read. Perhaps *defied* to read is closer to the mark. For the highest recommendation of the school text is not the degree to which it invites reading, but the degree to which it resists destruction. Now that school bookrooms are full of antique evidence that the battle for longevity has been won, we might next turn our attention to fresher evidence of the losing battle for literacy.

Just as the apparent isolation of the English teacher teaches the practical child to undervalue her subject, so does the forbidding ugliness of her texts teach him to ignore her materials. Innumerable children have told countless teachers that they don't like their textbooks, that they are afraid of their textbooks, that they don't read their textbooks . . . and the message has always been translated into impossible children rather than impossible textbooks. If we assume that the original translation has caused long life in textbooks and quick death in readers, and if we are serious in our desire to reverse the result, we might at least consider the possibility of a mistranslation. Perhaps textbooks are impossible, not children.

If we can remedy the sickness of the English teacher by enlisting outside aid, we may be able to do the same for her textbooks. Instead of merely going beyond the English classroom, however, let us this time go beyond the confines of the school. Anti-literate children, having learned to distrust the small, painful world of the classroom, are likely to invest what little trust they have in the larger world outside. Though they may never read magazines or newspapers, much less paperbound books, they regard all three as representations of a real world outside rather than products of an unreal world inside school walls. A child who can neither be induced nor threatened to read a school text, can often be drawn to the act of reading by the very presence in the classroom of newspapers, magazines, and paperbound books. Furthermore, the apparent relationship of his texts to the real world may convince him that reading in school is to some greater purpose than the accumulation of right answers and the approbation of his teachers.

Whereas the first hypothesis is relatively easy to argue because of its inclusion within the present context of public education, the second is not so easy to examine: "Literacy may not satisfactorily be taught in school to children caught between opposing forces of an adversary culture." Where two adversaries face each other, their confrontation can only be ended by change in one or both of their postures. No one familiar with the history of change in the schools can expect significant alteration in that adversary. It is the status of literacy in the community that must change before there can be hope for the education of the impoverished child.

The ultimate effect of this hypothesis, if proved, is not to absolve the schools from their responsibility for teaching functional literacy. Rather, it is to place that responsibility within the context of reasonable expectation. So long as school and community face each other in adversary stance, the school will do what it has always done—strengthen its walls rather than broaden its entrances. It becomes a fortress to protect rarified forms and values which cannot survive in the thick air of neighboring communities. And it becomes the isolated home of isolates like the English teacher.

What remedy for the disease of anti-literacy as it is bred in the school and nourished in the community? When formed in this fashion, rather than in the neater molds of teachers and materials, the question of literacy assumes something like its true proportions. Our common assumption has always been extraordinarily comforting: Effective classroom education is the right key for unlocking the word hoard of voiceless children. We must recognize now, I think, that we have been feeding on false hope. Our unexamined belief in the schools—a belief modified only a little by evidence of failure—has led us to regard the classroom as entirely necessary and largely sufficient to the task of forming community literacy. However we may regard the classroom and literacy, it is time we realized that significant portions of the impoverished community now regard both as deadly enemies of their self-regard and self-preservation.

6

THE SECOND PART of this book began by draw-
ing a limited parallelism between symptomatic diagnosis of
diseases like schizophrenia and linguistic impoverishment.
In closing this section now, I should like to draw a further
likeness—this time between treatments rather than diag-
noses of the two diseases.

A group of American psychologists has developed a
method for dealing with childhood schizophrenia which
may offer hope for rescuing some children from a fearful
wilderness. The method is based upon inexorable application of punishment and reward: A seven-year-old boy, later
diagnosed schizophrenic, retreats into a world of grotesque
destruction and grimace the moment each morning that his
father leaves home. His violent insanity drives his mother
into deep depression, his father into despair. Put him away?
Perhaps. But first, impossible as it may seem, punish him.

The theory behind the act of punishment is this: Enlight-
ened treatment of childhood schizophrenia, like that of most
other mental diseases, has depended upon professional
analysis of basic causation. In the case of schizophrenia,
with little professional agreement on the relationship

between influences of heredity and environment, effective treatment has been most remarkable by its absence. Let us recognize our ignorance of causation, argue the punishment-and-reward psychologists, and take the only positive action available to us. Unable to treat the cause, we can at least treat the effects. When the child's actions are socially unacceptable, punish him. Punish him by yelling at him, shaking him, spanking him, even slapping him. Punish him by withholding his pleasures—even food. Punish him by *paying attention* to everything he does and by demanding normality from him. When he conforms to your demands, be as attentive in reward as you were in punishment. The "cure" that may result from such treatment is not likely to be a cure at all, for the disease may only be in exterior control. Neither the child, given the opportunity to lead a useful life in society, nor society, is likely to care about the difference.

Another group of American psychologists has a viewpoint which results in treatment dramatically opposed to that of the first group. Bruno Bettelheim speaks for the opposition when he argues that "a spanking achieves a short-range goal, but it has a price tag—degradation and anger—that I am not willing to pay. My task is to build up self-respect. And I believe people do the right thing not because they are scared to death, but because their self-respect requires it."

Therapists who take this point of view would prefer that a schizophrenic child urinate in the middle of a room or on a crowded sidewalk rather than use the toilet through fear of punishment. And children who use physical violence are pacified rather than punished while the therapist attempts to search out and dam the child's wellspring of violence. Looming massively behind this permissive approach is the conviction that no sick child can be restored to society unless and until he participates in his own rehabilitation. If gentle and unvarying *attention* can bring the child to believe that someone cares about him, he may be brought to care about himself.

Add to punishment and permissiveness the view of another kind of illness held by psychiatrist William H. Grier, co-author of *Black Rage*. Grier agrees that the self-destructive sickness of black communities in America is a general response to the disease of second-class existence. But he also argues that this urge to self-destruction is a highly selective response to the real desires of the white community. Perceiving his true role in a slave society which is now embarrassed by the presence of its former chattels, the black man performs his last service for his white masters by attempting to exterminate himself. Just as the schizophrenic child, he can withdraw no further.

All three of these examples are of man *in extremis*. Suicide has forms worse than physical self-destruction; when a man (or child) is driven past his body into his mind by irresistible forces of personal and/or public disease, the counterforce must be equally extreme. When Willie Loman is slipping out of life in *Death of a Salesman*, his wife cries to their sons that "attention must be paid!" It is this rallying cry that relates the work of the punishing and permissive therapists as nearly as fingers on the same hand. The results of their work testify to nothing so much as the remediative quality of devoted attention. By desperate contrast, the results of dedicated inattention are as clear in the black man at the bottom of American society as they are in children of all colors at the bottom of American schools.

After rioting was finished in areas of two cities where I had friends amongst schoolchildren, I returned to those areas to listen to the children. Without exception, they claimed to have participated in the rioting; if they had not, they did not care to admit it to me. I learned very little of use to anybody. The children's descriptions of what happened are impossible to reproduce; without their faces and eyes, their moving bodies and hands almost unbearably excited—the words without their full accompaniment are flat and insufficient. One of their comments, however, will always remain with me. I heard it first in Detroit and again in Washington; the words were exactly alike:

"Ever'body gonna be lookin' at us now!"

Merely to be seen, for the invisible man, is a victory. Ralph Ellison understood that. So did those junior high school children 600 miles apart who knew that they and their families could be shot and burned but they could never again be ignored. ATTENTION MUST BE PAID. The implications of these few words are immense, and have yet to be fully examined by any social institution responsible for the welfare of invisible children. Of all such institutions, perhaps the school has done least to take those implications into account.

One form of attention which is particularly appropriate to the school is a dialogue, a true listening rather than a pause before speaking. A dialogue with school children who live in poverty uncovers a world of values that is largely ignored in American classrooms. For example, how is it to live in a world so ugly that clear sight of it would leave you blind? What accommodation with truth do you make if your instinct for survival is unimpaired and you can do little or nothing to change what you see? Suppose your father is besotted any time he has money enough to buy a bottle. What do you do in order to alleviate your pain? Though the answers to that question are as varied as the impoverished children who have such a father, they tend to have at least one element in common. For want of a better word, call it fantasy; or call it make-believe. Call it (if you're a schoolteacher) telling lies.

"My daddy? Take *two whole bottles* before he gone! 'At man pour it down like water. Ain't *nobody* can drink like my ole man!" Make a folk hero out of an alcoholic. Make a man out of your old man. Nobody knows as well as you do that your father is no better at drinking than he is at anything else. But speaking the truth can make the truth unbearable.

Telling lies and telling stories are not necessarily the same phenomenon. Telling lies can be an act of survival; telling stories can be an act of entertainment. In a barren world, conversation may flourish where other recreation is scarce. If you talk and you talk and you talk some more, you may be able to hang an opaque veil between yourself and boredom. In a life where nothing ever happens, one way to create the illusion of action is by talk. If, in the process, you don't tell it as it is, you have a temporary edge on a world that has a permanent edge on you.

What has this to do with the schools? No more than this: If teachers hold any pair of classroom values dearer than truth and decorum (silence), no one has yet discovered what those dearer values may be. The foundation of these values is the teachers' conviction that reproducing their own education depends upon training their students to keep quiet and tell the truth. It is time that teachers evaluated this double doctrine in terms of their pupils' needs as well as their own. It is time that they opened a dialogue with children-as-they-are instead of children-as-they-ought-to be. Such a dialogue would tell them that impoverished children sicken and die in the thin air of silence and the smog of truth-telling. Such a dialogue would also tell them that *attention must be paid,* or the children—like Willy Loman —will slip (or be pushed) out of life, forced over the edge by blows of blunt instruments like "Keep quiet!" and "Tell the truth!"

Biographical Note

Daniel Fader earned his bachelor's and master's degrees at Cornell University and his doctorate in English Literature from Stanford University in 1963. He is now an Associate Professor of English Language and Literature at the University of Michigan. As co-director of the project "English In Every Classroom," he was inspired to write *Hooked on Books: Program and Proof*, which has been acclaimed by teachers and lay persons alike. *The Naked Children* continues the chronicle of his passionate involvement in this project. Dr. Fader has also written numerous articles on literature and education. He has served as educational consultant for a number of companies, including University Microfilms, Inc., and the Xerox Corporation, and has been a consultant to the U.S. Office of Education.